The Poverty of Liberalism

The Poverty of Liberalism

By ROBERT PAUL WOLFF

BEACON PRESS   BOSTON

Copyright © 1968 by Robert Paul Wolff
Library of Congress catalog card number: 68–29314
First published by Beacon Press in 1968
First published as a Beacon Paperback in 1969
Published simultaneously in Canada by Saunders of Toronto, Ltd.
Beacon Press books are published under the auspices of the
Unitarian Universalist Association
International Standard Book Number: 0–8070–0583–5

Third printing, September 1970

To Patrick Gideon—as it turned out

The Poverty of Liberalism

1. Liberty

I

THE CONFUSION of contemporary American political thought shows itself nicely in the paradoxical fact that while liberals invoke the authority of John Stuart Mill's great libertarian tract, *On Liberty*, conservatives echo the rhetoric and deploy the arguments of Mill's other great contribution to social philosophy, *The Principles of Political Economy*. What is more paradoxical still, Mill's strongest arguments for what is today known as conservatism are set forth in *On Liberty*, a fact which liberals seem congenitally unable to notice; while in the pages of the *Principles*, we can find the germs of a justification of that welfare-state philosophy which modern conservatives abhor. As a radical, I view this conceptual chaos with a certain quiet satisfaction, but as a philosopher, I find myself irresistibly tempted to try some analysis and clarification, much as a doctor might feel his professional interest aroused by a particularly complicated case of cancer in his sworn enemy. I propose therefore to take a careful look at Mill's argument with particular attention to the fundamental assumptions on which it is based. I trust that my analysis will not merely strengthen the convictions of liberals and conservatives.

Mill sets for himself a quite precisely defined problem in *On Liberty*. What, he asks, are the nature and limits of the power which can legitimately be exercised by society over the individual? The question is moral, not political or historical, for it is the limits of *legitimate* constraint that Mill seeks. His answer, for which the entire essay is a defense, appears clearly and forcefully in the following lengthy paragraph:

> The sole end for which mankind are warranted, individually or collectively, in interfering with the liberty of action of any of their number, is self-protection. The only purpose for which power can be rightfully exercised over any member of a civilized community, against his will, is to prevent harm to others. His own good, either physical or moral, is not a sufficient warrant. He cannot rightfully be compelled to do or forbear because it will be better for him to do so, because it will make him happier, because, in the opinions of others, to do so would be wise, or even right. These are good reasons for remonstrating with him, or reasoning with him, or persuading him, or entreating him, but not for compelling him, or visiting him with any evil in case he do otherwise. To justify that, the conduct from which it is desired to deter him, must be calculated to produce evil to some one else. The only part of the conduct of any one, for which he is amenable to society, is that which concerns others. In the part which merely concerns himself, his independence is, of right, absolute. Over himself, over his own body and mind, the individual is sovereign.

All of *On Liberty*, running to well over one hundred pages, is devoted to sustaining this thesis. The actual argument is quite simple, and could have been stated by Mill in fewer than a dozen pages. The length and complexity of the essay are due entirely to the wealth of example with which he surrounds his proof. Nevertheless, as we shall see, the bare argument itself requires a good deal of analysis and criticism, for it is very far from establishing the proposition that Mill intended it to demonstrate.

Mill begins by distinguishing two spheres of activity and experience in each individual's life. The internal sphere includes the thoughts, feelings, and other experiences of private consciousness, together with those actions which affect —in the first instance—the individual alone. The external sphere is the arena of the individual's interactions with other persons, the social world in which we impinge upon others and influence their lives.

On this distinction Mill builds his argument. Society, he claims, has no right whatsoever to interfere in any matter falling within the inner sphere of any individual's life, and it has only a conditional right to interfere in social affairs involving interactions between several persons. In the latter case, society's guiding rule must be the principle of utility or greatest happiness principle. Society is to take action only in order to promote the greatest happiness of the greatest number. Where intervention will not serve that utilitarian purpose, society has no right to impose itself upon individuals.

In establishing this pair of principles governing society's relation to the inner and outer spheres of individual life, Mill proposes to rely solely upon the so-called Greatest Happiness Principle which he and Jeremy Bentham before him had made the cornerstone of the doctrine of Utilitarianism. Mill tells us that he will "forgo any advantage which could be derived . . . from the idea of abstract right." Other defenders of personal liberty had sought to buttress their position by appeals to "natural law," or "inalienable rights," or "the pure light of reason." They separated off certain rights of person and property as absolute, inviolable even by a justly constituted government. In this way they hoped to defend personal liberty against the powerful and ever-insistent claims of the state and its interests.

But Mill deliberately and with a touch of bravado rejects all such modes of argument. He will let his case stand or fall on the single principle of Utilitarianism. In the well-known essay of that name, Mill states his principle in the following manner:

> The creed which accepts as the foundation of morals "utility" or the "greatest happiness principle" holds that actions are right in proportion as they tend to promote happiness; wrong as they tend to produce the reverse of happiness. By happiness is intended pleasure and the absence of pain; by unhappiness, pain and the privation of pleasure. To give a clear view of the moral standard set up by the theory, much more requires to be said; in particular, what things it includes in the ideas of pain and pleasure, and to what extent this is left an open question. But these supplementary explanations do not affect the theory of life on which this theory of morality is grounded—namely, that pleasure and freedom from pain are the only things desirable as ends; and that all desirable things (which are as numerous in the utilitarian as in any other scheme) are desirable either for pleasure inherent in themselves or as means to the promotion of pleasure and the prevention of pain.

In short, whenever we face a choice among alternative courses of action—whether we be private persons or the authors of public laws—we should weigh as best we can the probable happiness and unhappiness to flow from each alternative, and then choose that course which promises the greatest happiness for the greatest number. For example, if we are laying down the penalties to be attached to crimes (a subject close to Bentham's heart), we must weigh the pain of the penalty against the happy prevention of future crimes which its infliction accomplishes. Somewhere between draconian severity and licentious levity will lie an appropriate schedule of punishments which achieves the greatest possible total happiness throughout the society as a whole. If the question be one of restraints upon business activity or the distribution of welfare supplements to indigent citizens, here too we must weigh the pains and pleasures and strive for a maximum of the latter.

Thus Mill sets himself the task of proving that the greatest happiness for the greatest number will flow from a policy of absolute nonintervention in the private sphere of human affairs, together with a policy of qualified interference in other-regarding or public actions, the qualifications to be the selfsame principle of Utility.

Now, if we begin with the assumption that every action by anyone whatsoever should aim at the greatest happiness for the greatest number, then of course it follows trivially that society's acts of constraints upon the individual, which are after all merely a sub-category of actions in general, should obey that principle. Hence the second half of the thesis requires no very great demonstration in terms of the assumptions of the essay. But the first half of the thesis, that society has no right at all ever to intervene in the private sphere of human experience, is obviously going to need something more in the way of argument. It is not surprising, therefore, that all but a small portion of *On Liberty* is devoted to this first proposition, which I shall for purposes of our discussion call Mill's Doctrine of the Liberty of the Inner Life.

According to Mill, *it follows from the greatest happiness*

principle that society must never interfere with an individ-ual's private life or self-regarding actions even for the pur-pose of making him happier! On the face of it, this is a very paradoxical claim. The total happiness of the society, we may suppose, is nothing other than the sum of the happiness of all the individuals in the society. Certainly Mill never gives us any reason to think differently. One would expect, therefore, that the very best way in the world to increase this social sum of happiness would be to interfere quite ex-tensively in people's lives, prodding them to do the things that will bring them happiness, stopping them from impru-dent or self-defeating actions which threaten to make them unhappy. Mill might, for example, succeed in persuading us that the forcible rehabilitation of drug addicts violates the civil liberties, natural rights, or dignity of the individual drug addict; on such grounds as those he might maintain that society has no right to interfere even in so hideously self-destructive a case. But can he really show us that it will reduce the sum of human happiness to cure addicts, even against their will? Clearly, some very powerful arguments indeed will be needed to establish so unlikely a claim.

II

Instead of making a direct defense of the Doctrine of the Liberty of the Inner Life, Mill begins by discussing one important instance of that doctrine, namely the liberty of thought and discussion. In a section fully one-third the length of the entire essay, he develops the famous argument for unconditional liberty of thought, speech, and writing. Most readers of *On Liberty*, indeed, are under the mistaken impression that freedom of thought and expression is the sole topic of the essay, and when modern liberals invoke Mill's name, it is usually in support of the right of a dissenter to speak his mind, or against the censorship of the written word.

Mill is uncompromising in his articulation of the principle to be defended. "If all mankind minus one," he asserts, "were of one opinion, and only one person were of the contrary opinion, mankind would be no more justified in silencing that one person, than he, if he had the power, would be in silencing mankind." Indeed, this absolute prohibition would remain valid even if we could be sure that the opinion were false, "We can never be sure that the opinion we are endeavoring to stifle is a false opinion," he reminds us; "and if we were sure, stifling it would be an evil still."

This is bracing talk, and the breast swells at the sound of it. But before assenting in an access of libertarian sentiment, let us consider Mill's arguments. The entire case, it will be remembered, is to rest on the estimation of future consequences and their tendency to promote the happiness or unhappiness of the members of society.

The proof depends upon the premise, unmentioned by Mill but clearly essential for the argument, that knowledge makes men happy. This Baconian presupposition must underlie any utilitarian defense of free speech which does not content itself with pointing to the pleasure derived merely from speaking one's mind. If knowledge does not tend to increase human happiness, then of course there is no possible utilitarian ground for protecting the institutions which conduce to the discovery of new truths. Inasmuch as there is an old Christian tradition according to which man's *unhappiness* in this world stems from his defiant tasting of the fruit of the tree of knowledge, one might expect Mill to make some effort to prove that knowledge brings happiness. Unfortunately, he makes no such attempt. Indeed, had he done so, he would have encountered a curious paradox which lies at the core of the utilitarian defense of free speech. The dilemma is this: Either an increase in knowledge tends toward an increase in human happiness, or it does not. If it does, then we ought to promote the growth of knowledge; if it does not, then we should stifle knowledge and strive to maintain a condition of happy ignorance. Now, the relation of knowledge to happiness is a matter of fact, not of principle, and cannot definitively be settled at any point in time. Hence, when we leave off speculating and make a social decision whether to allow free inquiry, we must perforce base our decision on provisional information. If the preponderance of evidence suggests that knowledge causes more unhappiness than it alleviates, then on utilitarian principles we ought to close down the research laboratories and universities, and content ourselves with repeating the old truths. To go against the evidence, to insist on the pursuit of knowledge even in the face of negative experiences in the past, would be to flout the dictates of utilitarianism, in the name perhaps of the sanctity of the truth or the inviolability of man's natural right to know. Now the paradox is clear. In order to decide whether we should permit the growth of empirical knowledge, we must settle a question which is itself empirical, and hence a very part of that knowledge whose value we are attempting to estimate. If we allow the question to remain open until it has been decisively settled, then by that very postponement of decision we have come down on the side of the advance of knowledge. On the other hand, if we close off investigation and opt for a static society, we deny ourselves additional data with which to improve our judgment on the issue. In short, so long as we restrict ourselves to the principle of utility, we cannot deal consistently with the question of the relation between knowledge and happiness. Hence, Mill's entire argument rests on an article of faith for which he advances no argument, and for which no utilitarian argument could suffice.

Lest this dispute appear a quibble, we might reflect that only twenty-five years ago, a number of the world's leading nuclear physicists seriously debated whether it was possible and desirable to forestall the development of nuclear weapons by banding together in a league of silence. Leo Szilard sought to persuade his fellow-scientists in the interests of humanity deliberately to refrain from pursuing the lines of investigation which, they had every reason to suspect, would shortly lead to the discovery of a practicable means for triggering a nuclear fission reaction. Szilard may have been too optimistic about his colleagues' ability to halt a major movement in physics, but it is a matter of historical fact that they made their recommendations to proceed to President Roosevelt only because of their belief that key German physicists had already begun the race for the uranium bomb. When we consider the history of the past quarter-century, can we so readily echo Mill's confidence that the advance of knowledge serves the enlightened interests of humanity?

If, for the sake of argument, we grant that knowledge contributes to happiness, we must still ask whether complete freedom of speech and expression is a necessary or even a particularly useful means to the advance of learning. Mill's arguments are familiar, and need not be rehearsed in detail: (Competition among ideas strengthens the truth and roots out error; the repeated effort to defend one's convictions serves to keep their justification alive in our minds and guards against the twin dangers of falsehood and fanaticism; to stifle a voice is to deprive mankind of its message, which, we must acknowledge, might possibly be more true than our own deeply held convictions). The root metaphor in all these arguments is of course that of the free market of ideas. Just

as an unfettered competition among commodities guarantees
that the good products sell while the bad gather dust on the
shelf, so in the intellectual marketplace the several competing ideas will be tested by us, the consumers, and the best
of them will be purchased. The American slang expression,
"I'll buy that!" as applied to a theory or idea exactly captures, albeit in a somewhat vulgar manner, the spirit of
Mill's vision.

Mill's arguments, like all utilitarian calculations of effects,
are estimates of probable future consequences. Since such
estimates rest upon past experience, it may be that we are,
one hundred years later, in a somewhat better position than
Mill to judge the usefulness of unconstrained discussion as a
spur to the advance of knowledge. Needless to say, even
now our conclusions can only be tentative, for as Mill himself repeatedly reminds us in his *Logic*, empirical judgments
are never certain. Indeed, we may wonder how Mill hoped
to ground an *absolute* prohibition against the limitation of
speech on merely *conditional* and *probabilistic* arguments.
But putting aside these methodological doubts, let us look
directly at the relation between freedom of speech and the
growth of knowledge.

Immediately it becomes apparent that we must make
some distinctions among different kinds of knowledge if we
are to throw any light on this question. Among the species
of actual or supposed knowledge which can be distinguished,
Mill pays particular attention to at least three, namely religious knowledge, scientific knowledge, and what might be
called moral or normative knowledge. I think a closer look
will reveal that the usefulness of free discussion to the advance of each of these species is quite different.

Consider first religious knowledge. I speak of knowledge
rather than of faith or belief because Mill is concerned with

the search for truth and the benefits it brings to humanity. We may ask two questions: first, will genuine religious knowledge bring human happiness? Clearly the answer is yes. Christianity—which we may, with Mill, identify as the relevant religion—promises eternal bliss, and threatens eternal torment. Nothing could be more important to a true utilitarian. Second, will a complete absence of restraints on discussion and advocacy offer the best chance for the discovery of religious truth? Here we encounter a paradox which has bedeviled religious liberals and nonreligious liberals alike. Christianity is a dogmatic, exclusive religion. It claims to have *the* truth about God, to offer through the savior, Jesus Christ, the *true* path to salvation. Faith, the precondition of salvation, is an unswerving trust in the promise of God. Now, a scientific belief might be compared to a financial investment—both are risks which one takes in hopes of a profit, ready at any moment to liquidate one's holdings if a better prospect offers itself. But faith is like love—only an irrevocable commitment holds the slightest chance of reward.

Thus there are two possibilities. Either I think there is not the slenderest argument or evidence for believing any religious doctrine, or else I see some reason, however shaky, for the commitment of faith. In the former case, I will be quite content to see religious debates go on, although I will not expect anything useful to come of them. But what of the latter case? What attitude should I take toward freedom of religion once I perceive some faint probability that one of the competing creeds is actually true? *If* the creed is true, then as we have seen I ought to be intolerant of all other creeds, for what each creed says is that it is the one true faith. And since each creed holds out the promise of infinite reward, any probability of its truth, however small, makes it rational for me to choose it and commit myself to it over all merely secular alternatives.* Hence, as soon as I see even a glimmer of a case for any religion, I ought on utilitarian grounds to commit myself to it unquestioningly and become completely dogmatic in my rejection of competing faiths.

On Mill's own principles, then, men who have no religious beliefs should favor religious toleration, while men who have any faith at all, however tentative, should be dogmatic, illiberal, and exclusionary. In short, religious liberty is a principle for agnostics, not for true believers. So far is Mill from having a convincing argument against religious bigotry, that his own principles actually encourage it in all those who have religious beliefs!

This paradox has of course long been a familiar fact of our lives, although it may not always have been formulated in quite this manner. Interfaith tolerance is always a sign of declining religious commitment. True believers, be they devout Catholics, orthodox Jews, or fundamentalist Protestants, are of necessity intolerant. The Catholic Church, to

---

* When the outcome of an action is uncertain, because several series of consequences appear probable to differing degrees, the modern theory of utility instructs us to evaluate the entire gamble, as it is called, by multiplying the values of the several alternatives by their probabilities, and then summing the products. The total is a discounted aggregate of the "expected value" of the action. For example, if I am offered five dollars for heads and ten dollars for tails in a coin toss, the value of the gamble is given by $(\frac{1}{2} \times 5) + (\frac{1}{2} \times 10)$, or \$7.50. This is the way a gambler calculates whether his chances are good or bad in a complicated game of chance. Now, the value of salvation to a utilitarian is infinite, even if he has declining marginal utility for bliss; and as every schoolchild these days knows, a fraction of an infinite quantity, however small, is still infinite. So, when a good utilitarian is offered a choice between the barest chance of salvation, on the one hand, and no chance at all on the other, then no matter how much fun he can have by shunning salvation, it is rational according to utility theory for him to seize the possibility of heavenly bliss. This is the mathematical basis for what Kierkegaard called the leap of faith. Needless to say, very few true believers are converted by these calculations, impeccable though they are.

its credit, resisted for a good many years the secular seductions of ecumenism, but the pressures of the modern irreligious world have finally forced it to succumb. As an agnostic, I welcome this decline in religiosity, but should I ever become persuaded of even the probability of religion, I shall with Mill's *On Liberty* in hand become as intolerant and persecutory as ever the Inquisition was.

The case of scientific knowledge also poses some problems for Mill's thesis. There is no doubt that the advance of science benefits humanity, excepting of course the development of weapons of mass destruction. But it is not so clear that scientific research demands an absolute freedom of speech and debate. Rather the evidence suggests that certain kinds of unfreedom place no obstacle in the way of science, while other kinds may indeed completely stifle fruitful investigation.

At any given moment, a scientific discipline is like a nomadic community moving through new and uncharted territory. There is a frontier along which exploration is taking place, a settled and well-established interior in which the accepted body of scientific truth is to be found, and a hinterland of old hypotheses, discarded theories, and exploded superstitions. Any obstacles placed in the path of those at the frontiers of knowledge, any restriction on the speculations they are permitted to project and the experiments they may perform, will most certainly inhibit scientific advance. So it was that Stalin throttled the science of genetics in Russia by requiring Soviet biologists to espouse the Lysenkoist theories of the inheritance of acquired characteristics. So too the liberal dogma of the identity of the several human races inhibits investigation of racially linked differential distributions of intelligence, susceptibility to disease, and so forth. And of course it is thus that science has been impeded by the religious objections which have from time to time been raised against new theories of astronomy, medicine, evolution, or psychology.

But it is not at all clear that any material harm can be expected from the suppression of those discarded theories which have been bypassed, and which are studied now only by philosophers or historians of science. Science is notoriously intolerant of its own history. No serious student of physics or astronomy wastes his time studying the writings of Aristotle, Ptolemy, or even Copernicus, Galileo, and Newton. Does anyone suppose that a bright young physicist must keep his belief in quantum mechanics alive by periodically rehearsing the crucial experiments which first gave rise to it? Is there a working chemist today who has at his fingertips the refutation of the phlogiston theory of combustion? It cannot have been such knowledge that Mill had in mind when he wrote:

> Even if the received opinion be not only true, but the whole truth; unless it is suffered to be, and actually is, vigorously and earnestly contested, it will, by most of those who receive it, be held in the manner of a prejudice, with little comprehension or feeling of its rational ground.

Orthodox science is "established" in our society in just the way that particular religious creeds have been established in earlier times. The received doctrine is taught in the schools, its expounders are awarded positions, fellowships, honors, and public acclaim; dissenting doctrines, such as systems of astrology, phrenology, divining, or clairvoyance, are excluded from places of instruction, denied easy access to media of communication, officially ridiculed, and—in the case of medical practices—even prohibited by law from translating their convictions into action.

Despite these restrictions, which in the case of religion are taken as the very stigmata of an unfree society, science flourishes and human happiness is advanced. It is hard to believe that even the most dedicated liberal will call for the establishing of chairs of astrology in our astronomy departments, or insist that medical schools allot a portion of their curriculum to the exposition of chiropractic in order to strengthen our faith in the germ theory of disease.

When we turn our attention to questions of morals and politics, Mill as it were comes into his own. The doctrine of religious liberty may be no more than a tactical maneuver by a nonbeliever to protect himself against the threat of official dogmatism; and the intellectual marketplace may not be an appropriate image of scientific activity. But in matters of collective social action concerning moral and political issues, the freest possible expression of competing views does seem called for. Even before we have reasoned out the principles underlying the right ordering of the political community, our instincts tell us that society is diminished by the arbitrary stifling of dissenting parties. Experience suggests that a vigorous competition of opposed policies, however disruptive of social tranquillity, is to be preferred to the enforced quiet of political repression.

Mill is right, or so we may provisionally grant. But is he right for the reasons he gives? Is freedom of political expression an efficient means to the discovery and preservation of some sort of truth or knowledge? If it is a matter of applying economic, sociological, statistical, or psychological knowledge to problems of taxation, urban planning, agricultural price supports, or mental health, then our discussion of science is more in point. Liberals do not object to the appeal to experts when social policy is to be implemented. But when it comes to debates concerning goals, norms, questions of value, then the very widest possible diversity of opinions must be actively encouraged. The doctrine of freedom of speech finds its natural application in distinctively political disputes about the principles of social justice and the goals of collective social action.

But it is not to assist the advance of knowledge that free debate is needed. Rather, it is in order to guarantee that every legitimate interest shall make itself known and felt in the political process. Every party to the decisions of government —which is to say, every citizen—must have the opportunity to argue his case and bring his pressure to bear. A voice silenced is a grievance unredressed or an interest denied a measure of satisfaction. Justice, not truth, is the ideal served by liberty of speech.

Indeed, it is just because norms and goals are *not* objects of knowledge, but rather of choice, that the greatest freedom of discussion with regard to them is necessary. If Plato were right, and Ethics like mathematics were actually a science, then there would be moral experts, and a frontier along which they advanced, and a hinterland of discarded doctrines that it would be neither fruitful nor desirable to keep alive.

The plausibility of Mill's doctrine of free speech derives almost entirely from the confused way in which his argument shifts from one sort of discourse to another. To the agnostic Mill, religious claims are neither true nor productive of human happiness, but precisely for that reason he would rather pay the cost of permitting free worship and proselytizing than suffer the social strains of interfaith warfare. Science is indeed a fruitful form of knowledge, but its advance requires only a limited freedom of speech, and the greatest benefit is actually derived from a systematic subsidization of the best established doctrines, to the detriment of those which have been discredited or discarded. Politics, finally, is not a matter of knowledge at all, but rather the arena of conflicting interests and competing social goals. Freedom of speech here is the indispensable medium of democracy, for it helps to protect individuals and groups against the tyrannical suppression of their legitimate concerns. It may be, of course, that the free expression of competing interests will advance the happiness of the members of society, although that depends at least in part upon whether it is happiness that they seek. But if so, it will not be by way of the increase of knowledge.

Mill, it will be recalled, forswore any advantage he might derive from an appeal to human rights, contenting himself with the utilitarian calculation of future happiness. I think it is now clear that Mill's tactic has failed, and that an adequate defense of free speech will after all be forced to invoke some notion of man's rights as a free and rational agent, rather than his satisfaction as a receptacle of pleasure and pain.

III

Our lengthy critique of Mill's defense of free speech has by no means exhausted the subject of the Liberty of the Inner Life, for it will be recalled that thought and expression are only a small part of that sphere from which society is to be unconditionally excluded. Leaving off consideration of special cases, we must now confront directly the doctrine of Individuality, or, as we may somewhat facetiously label it, the doctrine of the Sanctity of Idiosyncrasy.

Immediately we encounter a difficulty which crops up repeatedly in the writings of Mill: his noblest and most inspiring thoughts are almost invariably those which cohere least well with his professed utilitarianism. We have already seen that the absolute prohibition on censorship and the suppression of speech cannot successfully be supported by appeals to utility. It is notorious that Mill's distinction be-

tween higher and lower pleasures, although undoubtedly a
refinement of the rather mechanic sensibility of Bentham,
destroys the last vestige of plausibility of the utilitarian
calculus. Here too, we must ask whether Mill really intends
us to understand the principle of individuality as an infer-
ence from utilitarian premises, rather than as an independent maxim grounded in some natural human right.

If we take Mill at his word, we will interpret the principle of individuality purely as a theorem of utilitarianism,
for in addition to his initial rejection of any but utilitarian
arguments, Mill offers estimates of future happiness—or at
least of "well-being"—in defense of the right of each individual to live as he wishes so long as he does not infringe upon
the lives of others. On the other hand, the utilitarian defense of individuality is, as we shall see, even less convincing than the corresponding defense of free speech, and in
the *Principles of Political Economy*, Mill acknowledges a
series of exceptions to the principle so broad as to destroy
its force entirely. It would seem that here, as elsewhere,
charity dictates that we ignore Mill's professions and read
him as a libertarian in the tradition of Locke rather than
Bentham.

Nevertheless, I propose to hold Mill to his word, and
take seriously his attempts to ground the liberty of the individual in a calculation of utility. My purpose in adopting
this apparently unfriendly course is not polemic; more than
one great philosopher has developed an insight or proved a
principle despite himself, so to speak, and there is no wisdom to be gained from treating a philosophical text as
though it were a legal brief, making much of each slight
error or misplaced comma. Rather, I want to show that
when we attempt a strictly utilitarian defense of extreme
libertarianism, we very soon must acknowledge the weighty
empirical evidence which can be brought against it. And

when we then ask what new doctrine in place of libertarianism is called forth by the evidence, we find—or so I shall argue—that the natural answer is quite simply Welfare State Liberalism. In short, modern welfare liberalism and classical Millean libertarianism can be derived from the same philosophical presuppositions. They differ only in their evaluation of the facts of society and economy. Mill himself, in his *Principles,* can be observed shifting from one doctrine to the other as his evaluation of the evidence forces him to alter his doctrines. Modern American "conservatives" are merely nineteenth-century Milleans who have refused to admit the facts, and have elevated to the status of absolute and inviolable principles the doctrines which Mill sought to maintain on empirical grounds. That, indeed, is the reason why conservatives have fared so badly and liberals so well in the political arguments of this century. When two disputants agree on principles, and one denies the most evident facts while the other affirms them, it is not hard to predict who will win the argument.

Mill's argument requires that he prove three distinct propositions. First, he must show that there is a legitimate and reasonably sharp line to be drawn between self-regarding or private actions, belonging to the so-called inner sphere, and other-regarding or public actions, belonging to the outer or social sphere. Then, he must show that the cultivation and encouragement of individuality is, taking all in all, more conducive to human happiness than any set of legal and social constraints by which men's choices might be guided and their lives shaped. And finally, he must offer some evidence in support of the extreme dictum that absolute freedom from social interference is the best way of strengthening the growth of individuality and thereby of producing "the greatest happiness for the greatest number."

1   Let us begin with the inner-outer distinction. It is worth
quoting at length Mill's own account of the distinction:

> If any one does an act hurtful to others, there is a prima
> facie case for punishing him, by law, or, where legal
> penalties are not safely applicable, by general disap-
> probation. There are also many positive acts for the
> benefit of others, which he may rightfully be compelled
> to perform . . . In all things which regard the external
> relations of the individual, he is *de jure* amenable to
> those whose interests are concerned, and if need be, to
> society as their protector . . . But there is a sphere of
> action in which society, as distinguished from the in-
> dividual, has, if any, only an indirect interest; compre-
> hending all that portion of a person's life and conduct
> which affects only himself, or if it also affects others,
> only with their free, voluntary, and undeceived consent
> and participation. When I say only himself, I mean
> directly, and in the first instance; for whatever affects
> himself, may affect others through himself; and the ob-
> jection which may be grounded on this contingency will
> receive consideration in the sequel. This, then, is the
> appropriate region of human liberty. It comprises, first,
> the inward domain of consciousness; demanding liberty
> of conscience, in the most comprehensive sense; liberty
> of thought and feeling; absolute freedom of opinion and
> sentiment on all subjects; practical or speculative, scien-
> tific, moral, or theological. Secondly, the principle re-
> quires liberty of tastes and pursuits; of framing the plan
> of our life to suit our own character; of doing as we like,
> subject to such consequences as may follow: without
> impediment from our fellow creatures, so long as what
> we do does not harm them, even though they should
> think our conduct foolish, perverse, or wrong. Thirdly,
> from this liberty of each individual, follows the liberty,
> within the same limits, of combination among individ-
> uals; freedom to unite, for any purpose not involving

harm to others: the persons combining being supposed
to be of full age, and not forced or deceived.

(Initially, the distinction seems plausible) The image we
are invited to form is that of an individual alone in his own
home—his castle, as the English proverb has it—indulging
his tastes and gratifying his interests in ways which harm
no one save himself and which are not therefore properly
the business of either his neighbor or of society in general.
If he chooses to dress oddly, practice unfamiliar religions,
ruin his health with drugs, or squander his small income on
low pleasures, he hurts only himself; and if he persuades
other "consenting adults" to join him, who outside the circle
of participants can claim that his interests have been
affected?

Mill is aware of some of the more obvious objections to
the distinction, and adjusts his principle to take account of
them. For example, when a man has contracted with others,
as in marriage or business, his purely self-regarding actions
may take on other-regarding significance. One who through
suicide leaves his children destitute has injured them by his
act, despite the fact that it is his own life that he has taken.
Mill agrees that in all such cases, where explicit agreements
have given others the right to expect certain performances,
the inner sphere is contracted, and society may justly claim
jurisdiction.

The key to the distinction in Mill's several discussions
is the term "interest." I am liable to others when I affect
their "interests." Society may interfere only in those areas
of my life in which it has, or takes, an interest. Now this
distinction between those aspects of my life which affect
the interests of others, and those aspects in which they do
not take an interest, is extremely tenuous, not to say unreal,
and Mill does nothing to strengthen it. Mill takes it as be-

yond dispute that when Smith hits Jones, or steals his purse, or accuses him in court, or sells him a horse, he is in some way affecting Jones' interests. But Mill also seems to think it obvious that when Smith practices the Roman faith, or reads philosophy, or eats meat, or engages in homosexual practices, he is *not* affecting Jones' interests. Now suppose that Jones is a devout Calvinist or a principled vegetarian. The very presence in his community of a Catholic or a meateater may cause him fully as much pain as a blow in the face or the theft of his purse. Indeed, to a truly devout Christian a physical blow counts for much less than the blasphemy of a heretic. After all, a physical blow affects my interests by causing me pain or stopping me from doing something that I want to do. If the existence of ungodly persons in my community tortures my soul and destroys my sleep, who is to say that my interests are not affected? Since Mill himself assigns the pleasures and pains of the soul a superior rank over those of the body, he is hardly in a position to deprecate the spiritual suffering which the atheist by his mere existence inflicts upon the devout.

Naturally, we wish to reply that I take a *legitimate* interest in the safety of my person, while my interest in the private practices of my neighbors, however strong, is not legitimate and hence need not be taken into account when the public-private distinction is being drawn. But this answer, though appealing, is not available to Mill, for by ruling out arguments based on natural rights or a social contract, he has denied himself any a priori distinction between legitimate and illegitimate interests. From the point of view of utilitarianism, any potentially pleasurable event, act, or experience is a legitimate object of interest. The only ground of distinction permitted by utilitarianism is degree of pleasure or pain produced.

The root of the problem is that Mill treats the distinction between the inner and outer spheres as a matter of *fact,* whereas actually it is a matter of *rights* or *norms.* Self-regarding actions are those which only the individual himself has a *right* to concern himself with; his interests are the only interests which can legitimately be invoked in any moral evaluation. External or other-regarding actions are just those in which other persons have a rightful interest.

Oddly enough, after insisting so stringently on the reality of the distinction, Mill virtually gives it up in the course of replying to some of the objections which might be urged against his position. In Chapter IV of *On Liberty*, "Of the Limits to the Authority of Society over the Individual," he says:

> But with regard to the merely contingent, or, as it may be called, constructive injury which a person causes to society, by conduct which neither violates any specific duty to the public, nor occasions perceptible hurt to any assignable individual except himself; *the inconvenience is one which society can afford to bear, for the sake of the greater good of human freedom.* [Italics added.]

The argument contained in the last phrase is identical to that which would be put forward in connection with any *other-regarding* action. So Mill in effect admits that there is no factual difference in kind between actions of the inner sphere and actions of the outer sphere. Any action one cares to name may, under some circumstances, affect an interest which some other person holds; and conversely, any action, even that of murdering another or stealing his wealth, may fail to affect someone's interest. It is entirely a matter of the things men choose to take an interest in, and on Mill's principles at any rate, there is no a priori method for determining what they will be.

The second of the three steps in Mill's argument is the claim that individuality is a significant element—indeed, possibly the most significant element—in happiness or well-being. Mill himself is unclear about the precise nature of his claim. On some occasions, he seems to say that the free development of individual tastes and inclinations is a valuable *means* to the end of happiness. So he writes:

> As it is useful that while mankind are imperfect there should be different opinions, so is it that there should be different experiments of living; that free scope should be given to varieties of character, short of injury to others; and that the worth of different modes of life should be proved practically, when any one thinks fit to try them.

At other times, his language suggests that individual expression is *itself* a satisfying experience and hence one of the ends of life, not merely a means to some end. The truth, most probably, is that Mill personally valued individuality for itself, but felt it necessary to defend it to the world by a utilitarian argument. Certainly some persons at least derive pleasure from the mere experience of self-expression, just as most of us like now and again to make our own decisions even if we make them badly. Certainly, too, the consequences of unfettered individuality are on at least some occasions beneficial to human happiness. The matter reduces, therefore, to the *third* of Mill's claims: Is the encouragement of individuality, and with it the expansion of human happiness, best accomplished by an absolute prohibition against *all* social interference in the inner sphere of each person's life? Even assuming that we can draw a sharp line between inner and outer, will we maximize happiness by resolutely refusing to place constraints upon the most destructive actions, so long as they are *self*-destructive, and hence harmful only to the agent himself? Indeed, we may wonder whether the absence of all constraint is conducive to the development of individuality itself, or whether perhaps judicious social limitations upon individual action might not actually be a better way of nurturing a truly autonomous person.

Despite the importance of the principle of nonintervention and the unconditionality with which he formulates it, Mill offers very little in the way of support for it. Here is his principal argument:

> Neither one person, nor any number of persons, is warranted in saying to another human creature of ripe years, that he shall not do with his life for his own benefit what he chooses to do with it. He is the person most interested in his own well-being: the interest which any other person, except in cases of strong personal attachment, can have in it, is trifling, compared with that which he himself has; the interest which society has in him individually (except as to his conduct to others) is fractional, and altogether indirect: while, with respect to his own feelings and circumstances, the most ordinary man or woman has means of knowledge immeasurably surpassing those that can be possessed by any one else. The interference of society to overrule his judgment and purposes in what only regards himself, must be grounded on general presumptions; which may be altogether wrong, and even if right, are as likely as not to be misapplied to individual cases, by persons no better acquainted with the circumstances of such cases than those are who look at them merely from without. In this department, therefore, of human affairs, Individuality has its proper field of action.

In other words, everybody is the best judge of his own interests.

There are two ways of interpreting this claim, one of which makes it trivially true, the other of which makes it significant and, so far as the evidence is concerned, probably false. Looking at the question in one way, we might choose to interpret the notion of an "interest" behaviorally and dispositionally. That is, when we said that a man had a certain interest, we might *mean* that he characteristically pursued the interest, committed resources to it, made sacrifices for it, and generally evinced the behavior associated with it. On this interpretation, when we said that a man liked opera, or took an interest in it, we would *mean* that he attended opera performances, bought records of operatic music, read opera reviews, and so forth. If he merely *said* that he liked opera but did none of these things even when the opportunity presented itself, then we would conclude that he was misrepresenting his own interests. A man's failure to act in pursuit of some interest would be taken not as evidence that he did not know his own interests, but rather as evidence that he did not *have* that interest. So when the alcoholic went off the wagon, instead of saying that he lacked the will power to stick to his own best interest, we would say that his taking a drink showed that he really had a stronger interest in drinking whiskey than in staying sober. On the behavioral interpretation of interests, it is logically impossible for someone to choose against his interest, for his choice is *definitive* of his interest. So Mill's claim that each man is the *best* judge of his own interests would become the claim that each man is the *only* judge of his own interests. Since interest is defined in terms of choice, this is equivalent to the tautology that each man makes his own choices. A good deal of the plausibility of Mill's argument derives from our tendency to interpret it in this tautological way.

The alternative is to define interest in terms of happiness. To say that a man has an interest in remaining sober, for example, would be to say that he will derive more satisfaction or happiness from sobriety than from drunkenness. Thus interpreted, assertions of interest are empirical judgments which bear a contingent relation to the facts of choice. A man can perfectly well choose in a way which will fail to maximize his happiness or satisfy his desires. So the question becomes this: Taking into consideration all the evidence of past social experiments in constraint and freedom, and weighing as accurately as possible the probable consequences of alternative courses of social action, is the totality of happiness in our society likely to be greater if society interferes with the private lives and personal choices of its members, or if it keeps hands off and allows each man to live his own life as he sees fit?

So long as we confine ourselves to a case-by-case consideration of individuals, it seems plain that a bit of judicious meddling would considerably reduce the pain which imprudent persons inflict upon themselves; and of course, in the felicific calculus, a pain avoided is as good as a pleasure engendered. A drug addict who has successfully kicked the habit is thoroughly justified on utilitarian grounds in stopping some incautious young experimenter from taking the first steps down a road which may prove to have no turning. He knows, as the uninitiated cannot, how great are the painful consequences of true addiction in comparison to its undoubted pleasures. And if a friend, momentarily blinded by grief, thinks to take his own life, I may be better able to see that his future promises satisfactions which will in time outweigh the pain he is now suffering. Can I possibly be wrong, *on grounds of utility*, if I prevent him from destroying himself?

When acts as serious as suicide or drug addiction are under consideration, there is another sort of argument which is sometimes used to salvage the libertarian position. Individuals who commit such acts, it is said, cannot possibly be in full possession of their rational faculties. Hence they may be assigned to the same residual category as children, idiots, and madmen, and treated as wards of the society rather than as mature adults capable of self-determination. This argument has much in common with the familiar doctrine, now much in vogue, that antisocial acts are evidences of psychological derangement and should be treated medically rather than legally. A serious discussion of this argument would take us too far afield of our subject, but it is worth pointing out that once we allow societal interference with individual choice in all the really important areas of personal life, very little is left of the doctrine of the liberty of the inner life. Mill's position will count for nothing unless he is prepared to insist that a man has a right to make his own decisions at the risk of ruining himself or losing his life.

Mill's answer to this argument, of course, is that governments are not at all like thoughtful friends. Governments interfere with the lives of their subjects by means of laws backed by a monopoly of physical force. We cannot therefore settle the question of the limits of social constraint merely by reflecting on the actions of friends and relations. We must ask whether the evil consequences of establishing legal mechanisms of constraint and interference may not be worse, taking all in all, than the particular good which here and there results.

Whatever the truth about this murky matter, modern welfare liberals have again and again come down against Mill's claim that government interference causes more unhappiness than a strict policy of noninterference in the private sphere. Consider, for example, the problem posed by those persons too old or infirm to work. A good nineteenth-century liberal would argue, first, that each individual should be left to make his own arrangements for old-age pensions through voluntary private savings; second, that collective pension schemes should be privately organized and run; and third, that government action, if indeed it can be justified at all, should be limited to the establishment of a purely voluntary pension scheme which workers could join or not as they wish. Instead, of course, American liberals instituted social security, a forced-savings pension plan designed to protect individuals against the consequences of their own imprudence. Liberals judged, correctly no doubt, that those who needed a pension plan most would be just the ones not to join a voluntary plan and stick to it. The less money one has, the less likely one is to set a bit of it aside each week against the day, twenty or thirty or forty years hence, when one no longer earns a wage. A benevolent, interfering government took into its own hands a task which, on Mill's principles, should have been left to private individuals. The same decision has been made with regard to medical insurance and a host of other dangers which threaten the imprudent individual. Even in so private an area as the decision to smoke cancer-producing cigarettes, liberals today incline toward protective government legislation.

What distinguishes the modern liberal from Mill is the belief that greater happiness will flow from government intervention than from government abstention. The modern conservative, on the other hand, clings to the factual estimates made by Mill. That is why the *Principles of Political Economy* so often read like a Republican handout. It is indicative of the consensual stability of American politics that the two major strains of political thought agree in their fundamental principles and differ principally on a question of sheer fact. The absence of ideological rancor is traceable to this phenomenon, as is the superficiality of most political debates in contemporary America.

IV

When Mill turns to the question of the role of government in the public sphere, he offers a modified version of the classical liberal doctrine of laisser-faire. The subject is not treated in *On Liberty,* but in the concluding chapter of the *Principles,* entitled "Of the Grounds and Limits of the Laisser-faire or Non-Interference Principle," Mill makes his case. His general thesis is that:

> "Laisser-faire . . . should be the general practice: every departure from it, unless required by some great good, is a certain evil."

It is worth summarizing his particular arguments, for they remain the best statement ever made of the doctrine of classical liberalism, as well as of the philosophy of the Republican Party. Mill offers five principal reasons for limiting governmental authority and leaving as much as possible in the hands of private individuals.

First: every restriction on individual action "starve(s) the development of some portion of the bodily or mental faculties." Human well-being is furthered by the flowering of talents and the strengthening of individual faculties. But what the government does for a man he fails to learn to do for himself. As the pupil cannot learn to do his sums if the impatient teacher tells him the answer before he has had a chance to struggle with the problem himself, so an over-solicitous government, out of a commendable concern for the welfare of its subjects, may stunt the intellectual, spiritual, and cultural growth of a people by doing for them what they would better learn to do for themselves.

Second: each new task assigned to the government increases by so much its power and influence, and experience shows that those who possess power, even though they exercise it in the name of a majority of the people, tend to abuse their authority and "encroach unduly on the liberty of private life." Mill is as suspicious as any Midwestern conservative of central governments which gather into their hands the several reins of power.

Third: it is inefficient to burden an already over-committed central government with a multiplicity of tasks which it cannot adequately perform. The most elementary appreciation of the virtues of division of labor would lead one to see that social actions, if they are to be assigned to the government, are better distributed throughout a variety of bureaus at several levels of administration. On this point, we might remark, Democrats and Republicans have come to see eye to eye, and the current trend in Washington among welfare-state liberals is toward decentralization of such administratively complex affairs as the poverty program and aid to education.

Fourth: even well-organized governments tend by and large to do things less well than those persons whose interests are directly involved. It is generally true, Mill says, that "people understand their own business and their own interests better, and care for them more, than the government does, or can be expected to." What is more, a government which takes upon itself a task which might be performed by private individuals thereby deprives society of the skill and inventiveness of those individuals. Now, the normal workings of supply and demand tend to draw the best-suited individuals into the performance of any task for which there is a social need. If the government intervenes, at best it will employ those very same individuals, in which case there is little or no gain; and at worst, it will assign the task to less well-qualified persons, in which case society as a whole will suffer.

Finally, Fifth: the atrophy of intelligence and initiative which results from an overzealous government carries with it the gravest danger of political despotism. Democracy requires for its maintenance and health far more than merely a democratic constitution. The only defense of freedom is a free people, accustomed by practice and experiment to act for themselves. In a moving passage which, ironically, would be equally at home in the writings of Robert Taft or Paul Goodman, Mill voices this dedication to the supreme value of individual autonomy:

> The only security against political slavery, is the check maintained over governors, by the diffusion of intelligence, activity, and public spirit among the governed. Experience proves the extreme difficulty of permanently keeping up a sufficiently high standard of those qualities; a difficulty which increases, as the advance of civilization and security removes one after another of the hardships, embarrassments, and dangers against which individuals had formerly no resource but in their own strength, skill, and courage. It is therefore of supreme importance that all classes of the community down to the lowest, should have much to do for themselves; that as great a demand should be made upon their intelligence and virtue as it is in any respect equal to; that the government should not only leave as far as possible to their own faculties the conduct of whatever concerns themselves alone, but should suffer them, or rather encourage them, to manage as many as possible of their joint concerns by voluntarily co-operation; since this discussion and management of collective interests is the great school of that public spirit, and the great source of that intelligence of public affairs, which are always regarded as the distinctive character of the public of free countries.

What are we to make of this defense of laisser-faire? It is through and through utilitarian, which is to say that it rests on a series of empirical estimates of the probable consequences of different courses of action or inaction. Mill does not offer anything in the way of factual confirmation for his estimates, and in the absence of any method for measuring happiness and adding up pleasures and pains it is difficult to see how he could. Even in the face of a social catastrophe as great as a depression or war, a dedicated defender of laisser-faire could claim that less unhappiness was being caused than would result from government intervention. How would we even begin to decide such an issue?

The obvious suggestion is to take a vote. So long as everyone casts his ballot on the basis of a self-interested calculation of personal interest, something resembling a utilitarian calculus might emerge.* The objections to this proposal are rather technical, and an adequate rehearsal of them would require us to venture into the rarefied atmosphere of theoretical economics. Simplifying a good deal, the principal difficulty is that voting gives us no measure at all of the intensity of private interest, and since it is the sum of happiness and unhappiness that concerns us, intensity of concern is precisely what we most wish to measure. Suppose, for example, that ten percent of the population suffer extreme economic deprivation as the result of some institutional arrangement, while the other ninety percent gain a small, not very significant economic advantage from it. If everyone votes his interest, there will be an overwhelming majority in favor of retaining the existing state of affairs. The unhappiness suffered by the ten percent, if we could measure it, might far outweigh the slight gain in happiness for the ninety percent, but the vote could not show that fact. The minority would be forced to find some way, such as a riot, of

---

* Note that it is essential to the success of this proposal that everyone vote selfishly. If too many people, out of a misguided concern for the general good, vote for what they think will benefit society as a whole, then the result will be an *opinion* about the total happiness rather than a *measure* of it. As I have argued in Chapter 4, this structural constraint on individual concern for the social good is one of the principal theoretical inadequacies of welfare state liberalism. The system has a chance of working only so long as politics is an expression of private interests.

making the continuation of the status quo less desirable to the majority than a change. This, in effect, is what Negro slum dwellers in the United States have done, and viewed from the standpoint of liberal utilitarian democracy, their action is perfectly rational and quite legitimate.

Mill eventually realized that the policy of absolute nonintervention could not be defended on the utilitarian foundation he had laid. In the concluding portions of the very chapter in which the five-point defense of laisser-faire is elaborated, he acknowledges certain exceptions. Most of these consist of cases in which the factual assumptions underlying the noninterference doctrine turn out to be false. With admirable consistency, Mill thereupon admits that government regulation is justified, if not indeed virtually demanded by utilitarianism. Mill obviously views the exceptions as no more than minor adjustments of a principle which in the main is valid, but it is not difficult for us to see in his list the elements of a social philosophy much closer to modern welfare-state liberalism than to the individualism which he thought himself to be defending. In that sense, as I suggested earlier, welfare liberalism is a logical extension of the original libertarian position, which in turn is a deduction from utilitarianism rather than a doctrine of natural rights.

One of the exceptions, however, has a rather deeper significance, for, as we shall see, it hints at a non-individualistic conception of society and a thoroughly new theory of the role of collective action in pursuit of the general welfare. Mill himself seems to have been quite oblivious of the implications of his remarks, but with the hindsight derived from a century of development in social theory we can read into his observations a suggestion of the arguments which ultimately refute the most fundamental presuppositions of the entire liberal philosophy.

Mill distinguishes two sorts of cases of individual actions to which the principle of noninterference is supposed to apply. With regard to each category, situations arise which fail in some way to fit the assumptions on which the principle is founded; the exception is then a consequence of this failure. The first sort of case concerns the individual in his role as consumer, purchasing goods and services in the marketplace; the second concerns the individual as agent, making contracts, undertaking business ventures, and otherwise pursuing his interests directly rather than through the medium of the market. In general, as we have seen, Mill holds that the buyer is the best judge of what he buys; the buyer, rather than the state, can decide what interests he has and which commodities will best satisfy them. But the buyer is not always the best judge of the commodity, and if he is not, then quite consistently Mill concludes "the presumption in favour of the competition of the market does not apply to the case."

Oddly enough, Mill thinks that consumers are in general better judges of material than of spiritual or cultural commodities. When it comes to drugs, foods, soft and hard goods, Mill thinks we may confidently let the buyer beware, assured that he will, by and large, shun poor merchandise and encourage the good by his custom. Today, the almost universal judgment is that material goods are the commodities which consumers are *least* competent to judge. Who among us can tell whether an aspirin tablet is pure, or a can of clams contaminated, or a refrigerator improperly wired? In this, as in so many other cases, modern welfare-state liberals do not disagree with Mill's principles; they merely come to opposed conclusions about the facts. Characteristically, when conservatives argue today against government regulation of some commodity or productive process —for example, when ethical drug companies lobby against tighter federal controls on their products—they appeal to the same principle of utility and support their case both by citing the supposed ill effects which will result from regulation, such as a stifling of invention and enterprise, and by minimizing the dangers of unregulated commerce. As I remarked earlier, the victory of the liberals in one legislative battle after another stems not from any superiority of their political philosophy, but from the preponderance of evidence on their side of the factual dispute. A deformed baby traceable to an impure drug is a very strong answer to the general proposition that freedom from constraint stimulates experimentation and invention.

With regard to commodities of the mind, as it were, Mill adopts an unexpectedly paternal attitude. How similar in tone is the following passage to the animadversions against popular culture of writers like T. S. Eliot and Ortega y Gasset:

> But there are other things of the worth of which the demand of the market is by no means a test; things of which the utility does not consist in ministering to inclinations, nor in serving the daily uses of life, and the want of which is least felt where the need is greatest. This is peculiarly true of those things which are chiefly useful as tending to raise the character of human beings. The uncultivated cannot be competent judges of cultivation.

Mill goes on to apply this observation to the case of education, which he thinks ought properly to be provided by the government and required at least of every child, whether the parents agree or not. But an equally plausible application is to the subsidizing and censoring of the arts. There is here a conflict with the doctrine of absolute freedom of speech and expression, for many of the novels, plays, poems, and paintings whose aesthetic merits Mill would leave to the cultivated contain within them advocations and explorations whose aim is as much truth as beauty. Shall we ban some pornographic novel because it panders to inclinations which Mill and his fellow initiates know to be low, or shall we permit its publication because it espouses a deviant "philosophy of life" from whose barren roots may spring some flower of truth?

In a curious inversion of opinion which reflects a rising faith in technical expertise and a declining aristocratic confidence in matters of taste, the same liberals who rush to regulate drugs and dishwashers have shrunk from imposing their aesthetic convictions on the sweaty masses. As a concern for social welfare has pushed the federal government ever deeper into the business of regulating and guiding individual economic affairs, the legal constraints on artistic expression have been progressively removed.

Ironically, liberals intent upon defending the principle of free speech in the absolute version espoused in *On Liberty* have found themselves forced to use the sorts of utilitarian, elitist arguments more at home in Mill's *Principles*. If one takes *On Liberty* as a guide, for example, then the right of adults to indulge their lascivious desires by reading deliberately provocative pornography or by viewing lewd movies ought to be completely unregulated by government or society. Leaving aside the factual question whether the pleasure that one derives from such indulgence is greater or less than the pain which it might in some indirect way engender, the doctrine of the liberty of the inner life dictates that each person be left to make his own decision regarding so manifestly private a choice. An honest liberal, therefore, might be expected to go before a court and argue for the publication of *Fanny Hill* on the grounds that every man has a right to decide for himself whether he wishes to arouse his prurient desires by reading flowery descriptions of a variety of sexual practices.

Instead, we have over the years witnessed the less-than-edifying spectacle of a succession of literary critics testifying under oath that this or that book has "redeeming artistic merits" which override the unquestionably arousing character of some of its passages. So D. H. Lawrence is said to be a social psychologist and Henry Miller a moral philosopher. The natural consequence is that when some author or publisher, encouraged by the laxity of the courts, frankly seeks to minister to—pander to, we say—the desires whose secret satisfaction has swelled the sales of these literarily admirable productions, then the courts descend upon him with the wrath provoked by the failure of previous efforts at censorship. And appalled liberals find themselves stripped of arguments, for by their appeals to the criterion of literary merit, which is to say social usefulness according to superior standards of taste, they have implicitly forsworn the doctrine of absolute freedom of expression.

So much for commodities of the body and commodities of the mind. Now that psychiatry has achieved recognition as a legitimate branch of medicine, there is very little empirical ground for maintaining that the ordinary consumer is the best judge of the utility of either sort of commodity. If the liberal's inclination to regulate drugs is to be made consistent with his aversion to censorship, he shall have to find some other principle than Mill's utilitarianism on which to base his arguments.

The second category considered by Mill, though not so appealing to the literary mind, raises issues of much greater importance. We have to do here with cases in which there is no consumer whose choice in the marketplace determines the success or failure of some commodity, but where the individual as agent engages in some enterprise or activity either singly or through contract with other free agents. The general principle, Mill says, is the same here as elsewhere, namely that "most persons take a juster and more intelligent view of their own interest, and of the means of promoting it, than can either be prescribed to them by a general enactment of the legislature, or pointed out in the particular case by a public functionary." Nevertheless, Mill recognizes as many as seven sorts of cases in which government intervention can be justified.

Three of these categories of exceptions are of no very great significance for a general critique of the libertarian doctrine. Mill makes the usual bow in the direction of children and idiots (and, also, of course, the lesser breeds without the law—no man, it seems, can entirely free himself from the prejudices of his time), and sanctions as well a legal constraint on contracts which, however freely entered into, bind the participants in perpetuity. This latter exception takes in the practice of indenturing oneself as a servant, and also covers the case of marriage, on which Mill for well-known personal reasons took a strongly reformist line. A third set of excepted cases includes those in which the action to be controlled is one performed for the good of others. Charity, for example, since it is already a non-self-interested activity, might just as well be regulated by the state. Mill reasons that though we may generally expect each man to be the best judge of his own interests, there is no reason to suppose that private individuals will be better judges than the state of the interests of third parties. Again, Mill has in mind a particular social problem of his day, namely the Poor Laws of England, but it is not difficult to discern a very much wider application for this apparently trivial exception.

The next three headings carry us very far indeed into the camp of modern welfare liberalism. The range of cases which they cover is so broad that by the time Mill is finished sketching them, we may wonder where he imagines there is any room remaining for the doctrine of laisser-faire. The importance of this list of exceptions, needless to say, does not lie in the mere fact that Mill proposed them, nor that in doing so he seriously undermined his own position (I am not attempting to sketch Mill's intellectual biography, or to catch him out in textual contradictions). The real point is that by way of Mill's own limitations on the laisser-faire principle, we can see more clearly the connection between traditional and modern liberalism. The crucial point to remember is that laisser-faire is *not,* for Mill, a first principle or moral premise. The whole purpose of *On Liberty* is to *derive* the principle of noninterference from the moral axiom of utilitarianism. Mill's argument for noninterference is through and through empirical. Hence, when he recognizes facts which contradict the conclusions drawn in *On Liberty* he quite consistently limits the noninterference principle. As I have already remarked, in the realm of economics American conservatives defend as unquestioned axioms and first principles the very laisser-faire rules which Mill put forward as inferences from the doctrine of utilitarianism. American liberals, on the other hand, swear fealty to the memory of Mill, but draw non-laisser-faire conclusions from new and different facts. When it comes to the matter of free speech, the roles are reversed. Conservatives treat freedom of speech as a subsidiary principle to be forfeited whenever utilitarian considerations ("of national security") warrant; modern liberals, on the other hand, have long since elevated free speech to the sanctity of a dogma, forgetting (if they ever knew) that the classical liberal defense was empirical and utilitarian.

Before making some final attempt at sorting out this conceptual chaos, let us look briefly at Mill's three major exceptions to the principle of noninterference in economic matters. The first category concerns enterprises which, in their nature, can only be managed by delegated agency. When a

man launches some economic enterprise and personally over-
sees its direction, then Mill assures us he may be relied upon
better than the state to perceive and pursue his own best
interest. But if the enterprise must be placed in the hands of
others, *as in a joint-stock company*, then there is little to
choose between "private" and "public" management. In
either case, the individual is at the mercy of some other
man's estimate of his interests. "Government management,"
Mill writes, "is, indeed, proverbially jobbing, careless, and
ineffective but so likewise has generally been joint-stock
management. The directors of a joint-stock company, it is
true, are always shareholders; but also the members of a
government are invariably taxpayers; and in the case of directors, no more than in that of governments, is their proportional share of the benefits of good management, equal to
the interest they may possibly have in mismanagement, even
without reckoning the interest of their case."

Since virtually the entire American economy is now controlled by joint-stock corporations we may conclude that
Mill would endorse a program of strict government management of private business. The premises of individualism
quite naturally entail this collectivist conclusion: all that is
required is a recognition of the changed circumstances in
which the major portion of the economic activity of the
nation is conducted. Modern individualists, having transformed Mill's conclusions into a priori principles, are quite
naturally no longer able to argue for them. Mill, on the other
hand, is sufficiently aware of their original justification to
recognize their limitations. It is of course understandable
that he might fail in 1859 to see how deep his "exception"
cuts into the core of the individualist doctrine.

In the light of these reflections, it is interesting to note
that recent apologists of corporate enterprise have taken to
portraying the executives of modern joint-stock companies

as quasi-statesmen, motivated by an essentially political concern for the general good rather than by the traditional liberal virtue of unalloyed greed. To read Berle and Means, for example, one would imagine that the president of General Motors modeled himself on Max Weber's "ethic of responsibility" rather than on Benjamin Franklin's autobiographical reflections concerning the economic value of the appearance of honesty. There is, of course, a certain logic to this refurbishing of the portrait of the modern corporate executive. If, as Mill says, there is no essential difference between the delegation of authority and interest in a corporation and a government, then it may begin to occur to people to transfer that authority to men who have demonstrated some measure of competence in the art of representation. The natural defense against this dangerous conclusion is to claim that the authority is already in the hands of statesmen—corporate statesmen—and hence that no unsettling transfer of control is necessary. Perhaps the last word here may be given to Mill, who exhibits a quite unsentimental awareness of the political limitations of "people's capitalism."

> It may be objected, that the shareholders, in their collective character, exercise a certain control over the directors, and have almost always full power to remove them from office. Practically, however, the difficulty of exercising this power is found to be so great, that it is hardly ever exercised except in cases of such flagrantly unskilful, or, at least, unsuccessful management, as would generally produce the ejection from office of managers appointed by government. Against the very ineffectual security afforded by meetings of shareholders, and by their individual inspection and enquiries, may be placed the greater publicity and more active discussion and comment, to be expected in free countries with regard to affairs in which the general government

takes part. The defects, therefore, of government management, do not seem to be necessarily much greater, if necessarily greater at all, than those of management by joint-stock.

A second class of exceptions, Mill says, are those actions by individuals which, "though intended solely for their own benefit, involve consequences extending indefinitely beyond them, to interests of the nation or posterity, for which society in its collective capacity is alone able, and alone bound, to provide." Mill has in mind colonization, but here as in the previous case, a consistent application of his reasoning would extend the exception far beyond the limits he indicates. In a complex, highly integrated society, there are *no* economic actions, and scarcely any others, whose long-term consequences do not materially affect collective interests for which only the entire society can be responsible. Even so private an act as the conception of a child becomes part of a population growth whose economic and social consequences pose critical problems for the state. A policy of enforced sterilization would, on Mill's principles, be justified, indeed demanded, in situations like those which exist in many nations today.

This example is typical of all of Mill's exceptions to the rule of laisser-faire. What he sees as peripheral adjustments affecting such relatively minor issues as colonization turn out in fact to carry implications whose thorough working-out results in a total transformation of the responsibilities of the state and a major shift of emphasis from private initiative to government action. The underlying principles remain unchanged: Always act for the greatest happiness of the greatest number; and Never interfere with anyone save to serve the general welfare. But we begin to see that consistent obedience to these two maxims entails an enormously active state machinery and a considerable measure of social con-

trol. Thus is welfare-state liberalism born from the seeds of
classical laisser-faire libertarianism.

Mill's third major category of exceptions to the principle
of laisser-faire has an equally broad application in the conditions of contemporary American society. Whenever any
social need develops which, by some accident of the market,
fails to offer a profit sufficient to entice private capital into
its satisfaction, then he says, the government has a duty to
"make the work its own." Mill cites the mounting of scientific
explorations and the maintaining of lighthouses as instances
of this principle, but we are today familiar with considerably
more important social needs which come under the heading
of unprofitable enterprises. Good low-cost housing, for example, is desperately needed in the United States, but the
economics of the building industry makes it impossible for
capital to earn a high enough profit to guarantee the satisfaction of the need through the workings of the market.
The obvious solution is either to alter the economic prospect
artificially, through such measures as tax incentives, so that
a previously unprofitable opportunity becomes potentially
profitable; or else to invest tax money directly in the under-
capitalized sector through a program of public housing.

A number of commentators on society and economy, fore-
most among them John Kenneth Galbraith, have analyzed
the divergence of the market mechanism from the demands
of social utility. Over a broad and growing range of cases,
effective market demand bears no relation to manifest social
need. Theoretically schools, roads, parks, sanitation, police,
and even national defense could be provided in a capitalist
society by private firms drawn into production of goods and
services by the hope of a profit. But for a host of familiar
reasons America assigns these functions to government rather
than to private industry. During the protracted struggle between conservatives and liberals over the appropriate limits
of federal responsibility, the conservatives have repeatedly

lost because of their inability to show that private initiative could actually provide the desired commodity or service. In the peculiar political conditions of the United States, this dispute has been confused with the struggle between state and local government on the one hand and the national administration on the other. Since state and local governments are indisputably governments, it is very hard to see the logic in the conservatives' position. In fact, of course, the appeal to states' rights is an ill-concealed attempt to justify *inaction* rather than private initiative. If local communities actually showed themselves willing to provide the services now demanded from the federal government, there is every reason to believe liberals would be delighted.

It remains to be seen whether tax incentives and direct government spending can adequately correct the grotesque imbalance in America's investment of its capital resources. The principal obstacle to the success of these welfare-state techniques is not political opposition to them but the contradiction which lies at their heart. Absurd as it may seem, under the present system, if the economy is making too many cars and building too few schools, the only effective way to get more schools is to make yet more cars! Schools are paid for by taxes, which in turn are levied on profits and wages. If taxes are increased economic growth is stifled, and in the end a smaller amount of money actually comes into the government's treasury. So spending in the "public sector," as Galbraith has called it, is financed out of ever greater growth in the private sector. So long as the demands of the public sector are small relative to the economy as a whole, and needs in the private sector are being serviced by the general economic growth, the logical absurdity of this system will only bother philosophers. But the time is fast coming when the need for direct transfer of capital from the private to the public sector will make itself felt in the political life of the country. Enormous sums of money are

now being asked for such major public projects as the systematic reclamation of the central cities of America. The
question is not simply whether the private sector is large
enough to provide the tax revenues with which this reclamation is to be accomplished, but whether it makes any social
sense at all deliberately to stimulate the sectors of the economy which are already out of balance in order to ensure the
profits and wages from which the taxes will come. How
many cars must we build in order to pay for a central city
from which the car is banned?

V

We have come a long way from the simple maxim that each
man is the best judge of his own interests. Even if the doctrine of noninterference in the private sphere could be defended on utilitarian grounds—and in the first sections of
this essay I indicated why I think such a defense must fail—
the more general rule of laisser-faire in regard to the public
sphere clearly cannot be derived from the Greatest Happiness Principle. Nevertheless, as I have tried to show, the
movement from the individualism of *On Liberty* to the welfare-state liberalism of the final sections of the *Principles of
Political Economy* involves no fundamental revision of the
assumptions underlying Mill's social philosophy. He remains
in the *Principles*, as he was in *On Liberty*, committed to a
utilitarianism which, in its conception of human happiness
and social relationships, is methodologically individualistic.
In the final essay of this book, I shall try to suggest a foundation on which a radically different conception of social goals
and human relationships might be grounded. At this point,
I wish only to indicate a way in which Mill himself acknowledges the inadequacy of the individualist model. The hint
is contained in the last of the exceptions to the laisser-faire
principle.

There are some matters, Mill notes, "in which the interference of law is required, not to overrule the judgment of individuals respecting their own interest, but to give effect to that judgment." This happens, he argues, when the end they seek requires them to concert their actions in a way which is rational for each only so long as he can be sure of the cooperation of all. Mill cites the instance of a group of workmen who seek to raise their wages. Under the conditions of a market economy, if any individual by himself demands higher wages, he merely prices himself out of a job and is replaced by a competing worker who accepts the lower wage. But if all the workers unite and collectively insist upon a raise, then they can make their wills felt and achieve their end.*

Familiar as Mill's point is, we ought not to ignore the full power of its implications. Until now, Mill has been dealing with enterprises which are individual in their nature, however much they may be influenced by the behavior of others. Here, for the first time, he recognizes the existence of activities which, at least in a certain limited sense, are inherently social or collective. He is on the edge of formulating Marx's central thesis that human production is social in its nature and hence cannot be correctly analyzed by the individualist model of classical economics. To be sure, Mill still sees the relationship among the several workers as purely instrumental in character; to each individual worker, the activities and satisfactions of the other workers are important only as means to his own satisfaction. But he begins to see that in the pursuit of their private ends they may be so bound together that they sink or swim collectively.

---

* One would have thought that this simple lesson of the necessity of labor solidarity would by now be as well known as the roundness of the earth, but there are still a great many salaried employees, notably on the faculties of universities, who seem not to grasp its simple logic.

Insofar as our enterprises are inherently social, the public-private, interference-noninterference model of human relationships breaks down. The central problem ceases to be the regulation of each person's infringement on the sphere of other persons' actions, and becomes instead the coordination of the several actions and the choice of collective goals. It would be madness, for example, to suppose that the basic problem for a string quartet is to determine where the rights of the first violinist end and the rights of the cellist begin. For the quartet, the real problem is to achieve harmonious interaction. Now, of course, disputes arise which require resolution—for example, what composition to play. But these are not disputes over infringements of individual liberty, and they must be settled by some technique of collective decision-making, not by arbitration and the guarantee of mutually self-regarding liberty.

The collective character of social action is the universal presupposition of the social sciences, and modern liberals, who have wholeheartedly adopted the theories of sociology and social psychology, are accustomed to view society through the eyes of conservative social theorists like Weber and Durkheim and radical social theorists like Marx. Despite their assimilation of collectivist sociology, however, liberals continue to employ the assumptions and models of an individualist politics. The result is a confusion which contributes to the incoherence of contemporary political discussion in the United States. In the essays which follow, I shall return several times to this conflict between the political convictions and sociological theories of liberal social philosophy. It is a measure of Mill's perspicacity, and also a revelation of his limitations, that he should in his own writings have reflected the contradictions which haunt liberalism a century later.

2. Loyalty *

THE DIFFIDENT AND INEFFECTUAL RESPONSE of American liberals to the attacks of the political right in the 1950's revealed a deep confusion over the concept of "loyalty." Liberals were uncertain about the propriety of the federal loyalty and security program, and confused over the legitimacy of judging a man's loyalty by his "associations." The government itself seemed not to know what was meant by "loyalty to the United States." The standards of loyalty defined by the various executive orders were either vague or else hodgepodges of inspirational exhortations and injunctions against acts which were already crimes under existing laws. The questions raised by the loyalty program were many and difficult to answer: Could a man have done nothing for which any court might try him, and yet be disloyal to his country? Should the determination of loyalty be a quasi-legal procedure subject to the restrictions of due process and protected by constitutional guarantees? Were a man's tastes, interests, personal associations, or family ties relevant data for a judg-

* This essay is an expanded and revised version of "An Analysis of the Concept of Political Loyalty" in my *Political Man and Social Man*, © copyright 1966 by Random House, Inc., and used here by permission.

ment of loyalty? Was loyalty anything more than the mere
negation of disloyalty?

The literature provoked by the loyalty crisis discussed
the issues heatedly but without very much illuminating
them. At first, liberals merely defended from attack anyone
whom they conceived as a kindred spirit. The philosophical
foundations of the response seemed to extend roughly to
the principle, "The enemy of my friend is my enemy." The
very same people who ridiculed Midwestern superpatriotism
insisted that the suspected security risks were as patriotic,
as loyal, as any American Legionnaire. One and the same man
would be praised for his loyalty *and* for his willingness to
place principle above country. In all, the showing of American liberals was not one to inspire admiration. There were
acts of courage, but very little intellectual clarity about the
principles which dictated them. In a way, we might say that
the root problem was *conceptual* rather than *moral*. The idea
of loyalty was so obscure that even those men willing to
stake their reputations and fortunes on a matter of principle
found it difficult to discern just what acts their principles
required.

In this chapter, I try to advance debate on the problem of loyalty by developing a conceptual analysis of the
idea before plunging into direct argument on the substantive
issues of the dispute. The discussion, particularly in the first
several sections, may seem overly abstract and refined. After
all, as Aristotle wisely remarks at the beginning of his
treatise on ethics, there is nothing to be gained from trying
to achieve greater precision in an investigation than the subject matter will allow. Nevertheless, I hope to show that
some of the most tangled questions, including the disputes
over loyalty oaths and guilt by association, can be cleared
up through the application of the results of the analysis.

I

What is loyalty? We can hardly decide whether the state
has a right to demand it of its citizens, or what evidence of
it ought to be allowed in courts, until we become somewhat
clearer about what we mean by the term. Perhaps the best
way to approach the problem is to ask what we mean when
we say of a man that he *is loyal.* There are at least four quite
distinct things that we may be saying about a man when we
call him loyal.

First, we may mean to attribute to him a certain disposition of character, much as we might say that he was courageous, or generous, or industrious. In other words, people
who speak of loyalty or demand it of American citizens may
have in mind a certain personality trait. Now, character traits
are habits of behavior, or propensities to act in certain sorts
of ways. When we say that a man is courageous, for example, we mean that he tends to do such things as stand and
fight when attacked on the battlefield, or endure pain when
it is necessary, or risk his life in the performance of his duty.
Similarly, we call a man generous if he exhibits a propensity
for sharing his wealth with his friends. Of course a man
need not take *every* opportunity for bravery in order for us
to consider him brave, any more than he need give away all
he has in order to be truly generous. But if his behavior, over
a long period of time, exhibits a certain *pattern,* we attribute
courage or generosity to him.

The ascription of a personality trait to a person is at one
and the same time a description and a prediction. When we
call a man brave, we are saying that he has in the past ex-
hibited some of the behavior which we associate with courage, and that in at least some of the situations which might
arise, he will continue to do so in the future. Like any other

description and prediction, the ascription of a personality trait is based on past observations in conjunction with some general knowledge about human nature. He has done thus and so, we say, and that, together with other things we know about him, shows that he is the sort of person to do similar things in the future. Needless to say, such empirical estimates are fallible, but like all empirical estimates they are capable of being improved by additional evidence.

Philosophers have offered two different analyses of the relation between a character trait and the individual acts associated with it. On the simpler, and older, view the character trait is an internal state of the self which causes the individual to act as he does. To say that a man *is* courageous is to say that he possesses a certain strength of personality or moral set, whether he actually reveals it or not. Then, when he stands firm in battle, we *explain* his brave action by saying that it was caused by his courage. Viewed in this way, brave acts are evidences that courage is present in the individual, much as a temperature is evidence of an infection or the smell of rotten eggs is evidence of the presence of hydrogen sulphide.

Recently a number of philosophers have shown that this picture of character traits is a logical confusion, based on the false notion that the self is some sort of entity which lurks inside the body and moves it about like a puppet. They argue that courage, for example, simply *is* the disposition to exhibit certain sorts of behavior. "Courage" is not the name of an internal state of the mind which produces brave acts; it is the name of those acts themselves, or rather the name of the disposition to commit them. Understood in this way, courage is rather like gracefulness. Just as it doesn't make any sense to say that a man walks, sits, stands, and dances gracefully, but is *really* clumsy inside, so it doesn't make any sense to say that a man stands firm in battle, endures pain, and risks his life in the line of duty, but is *really* a coward inside.

How shall we describe the character trait called loyalty? First of all, a loyal person is loyal to something. The proper object of loyalty is either another person, a group of persons, or an institution. The loyal man comes to the aid of the object of his loyalty when its interests are threatened; he identifies himself with its career, making its successes his successes and its enemies his enemies. He is prepared to sacrifice for it, even to the extent of giving his life in order that it may be safeguarded. The loyal man takes pride in his loyalty object and expresses solidarity with it through ritual acts which evoke and reinforce his emotional identification with it. Frequently he focuses his feelings through symbols such as a song, a flag, or a name.

Strictly speaking, loyalty conceived as a personality trait is the disposition or tendency to exhibit a pattern of action which includes many of these particular acts, and others besides. The appropriate evidence for an ascription of loyalty (or disloyalty) would be past acts together with such general knowledge of human behavior as allows us to predict future actions. Since loyalty, thus conceived, is a disposition to a certain *pattern* of behavior, a broad diversity of evidence would be relevant to it. Legally, the best sort of supporting testimony might be "character witnesses" who could establish the existence of the appropriate pattern by recounting incidents from various periods in the subject's life. In short, loyalty-as-a-personality-trait would be demonstrated in just the manner that we would prove someone to be courageous, generous, or thoughtful. Later on we shall have to ask ourselves whether a court of law or security board is an appropriate place for deciding such a question.

In addition to the concept of loyalty as a character trait, there is a second sense which is sometimes intended when a man is called "loyal." We may mean to ascribe to him a certain status as defined by law. The notion of a legal status needs elucidating, for it is neither descriptive nor normative, but what has been called "ascriptive" in character. When we say that a man has killed someone, we assert a causal connection between some act of his and the other's death. But when we call him a murderer, we are strictly speaking asserting that a duly constituted court of law has tried him for the crime of murder, that it has found him guilty, and perhaps also that he has appealed and lost. In short, the term "murderer" is a legal term, and we use it to ascribe a legal status to a man, one which makes him liable to certain punishments and disabilities determined by law. A killer who has been acquitted is not a murderer, in the proper sense of the term. When we call him such, we usually mean that he is morally reprehensible and deserves to be punished in the way that the law customarily punishes murderers. Speaking quixotically, we mean that he ought to be a murderer—ought, that is, to have the legal status of murderer imposed upon him.

The notion of a legal status is easily illustrated from the law of property. The thought which first comes to mind when one thinks about property is that ownership is based upon some natural relationship, such as actual physical possession, as when a squatter claims to own the land he sits on or as in the saying "possession is nine points of the law." But a little reflection reveals that there is no natural relation between a man and a piece of land, object, or economic right, which is either sufficient or necessary to his ownership of it. To own something, it is not necessary to have one's hands on it, nor even to be in its vicinity. One can own something without ever having seen it, or even knowing of its existence. Ownership usually does not carry an absolute right to do with the property as one wills, or to destroy it if one chooses. Ownership is a complex set of legally determined rights and responsibilities which cannot be reduced to a natural relationship. The legal fact of ownership is determined by a court of law, just as is the status of murderer. The court does not discover ownership; it determines it, in the proper sense of the term. Until the court has handed down an opinion, there is strictly speaking no ownership at all. Here again, however, we may assert moral principles which we believe ought to find expression in the laws of property. A classic example is John Locke's argument that a man gains a proprietary right to an object through mixing his labor with it and fitting it for human use.

The interpretation of loyalty as a legal status has historical antecedents in the medieval concept of a "legal" man, which is to say a man who was entitled to appear in court as a free man, possessed of the full rights and protections of the law. A legal man was contrasted either with a serf, who could not for example serve on a jury, or with an alien, who stood outside the normal processes of law. In modern times, as in classical Athens, the concept of legality is submerged in that of citizenship, or perhaps "full" citizenship, to distinguish it from the disadvantaged status of criminals and others who have lost some of their political rights. On this interpretation of "loyalty," then, to say that a man is loyal is to say that he is legally a citizen in good standing, and fully possessed of the rights of citizenship as defined by law.

Loyalty so understood is a status to be ascribed by the decision of a legal or quasi-legal body. As a man in medieval England might go to law to establish that he was a free man and hence entitled to own land, marry whom he chose, or inherit property, so an individual accused of disloyalty would come before a court to have the charge adjudicated. Calling a man disloyal would, in the first instance, be equivalent to asserting that he had been denied the status of citizen for one or more of a number of specified causes. In a precisely analogous manner, when we call a man an alien, we assert that he has a legal status and imply that it has been ascribed to him (by law) for one of the causes laid down by law (such as foreign birth, conflicting citizenship, falsification of naturalization papers, etc.). Needless to say, we may charge a man with disloyalty just as we may charge him with murder, meaning thereby that by his acts or omissions he has in our opinion earned the status of "disloyal." We may by extension mean that although the law does not now proscribe such acts as his, it ought to do so. But strictly, to call a man disloyal is to assert that he has been adjudged disloyal by an appropriate tribunal. Loyalty, on this second interpretation, is precisely what the law says it is.

In yet a third sense, "loyalty" may also mean "orthodoxy" with regard to some set of political or philosophical principles. Calling a man disloyal can be a way of saying that he has dissented from a dogma or perhaps merely that he has failed to confess it with sufficient frequency and vigor. Disloyalty is thus assimilated to heresy or apostasy.

As with religious orthodoxy, so with the political variety. The creed may consist either of factual assertions or of moral principles. The loyal man is one who believes *that* the assertions are true, or who believes *in* the principles. In political life, there is no limit to what may come to be either a test or a component of doctrinal loyalty. To be a loyal American, on the view of some people, one must believe that the theory of laisser-faire capitalism is an adequate analysis of industrial life. Others demand that one believe in the equality of man, which still others interpret as the belief that intelligence is not genetically linked to skin color.

It is useful for analytical purposes to treat the identification of loyalty with orthodoxy as a distinct meaning of the term, but its connections with the first two meanings are of course very close. Beliefs, as motives of action, are evidence for the existence of character traits, though experience teaches us not to take them at face value without some corroborating support from behavior. Beliefs also may be among the criteria for the ascription of a legal status. The history of religious persecutions has made Anglo-American law wary of test oaths and other enforced expressions of belief, but in principle there is no legal impossibility in requiring a confession of faith as a condition of obtaining or preserving one's status as a citizen. (The oath of allegiance is not such a confession, as we shall see presently.)

The last and most important sense of loyalty is that of remaining true, being faithful, honoring a moral commitment. This is probably the most common use of the term today, as well as its original meaning. Loyalty as the honoring of a moral commitment must be distinguished from loyalty as a character trait, though the two are obviously very closely related. To have a character trait is to be disposed to respond in certain ways to situations of a specific type. These responses are spontaneous and issue from inclination, not an awareness of duty. A man may be of a faithful disposition without having contracted a moral commitment to the object of his loyalty; conversely, he may loyally fulfill his obligation without feeling an unforced inclination to do so. Some philosophers argue that in fact the fulfillment of moral commitments—the doing of one's duty—psychologically must involve habits of character. Aristotle and Plato may both be read in this way. But since the concepts of loyalty as a disposition and loyalty as the honoring of a commitment are logically distinct, it is as well for our purposes to treat them separately.

There are many sorts of moral commitments, and most are not entitled "loyalty." Strictly, men are said to be loyal either to individuals, to groups, or to institutions. By extension, we sometimes speak of being loyal to a principle or an ideal, and some philosophers have made a great deal of this sort of abstract loyalty. I shall not treat it in this essay, save insofar as it can be subsumed under the heading, loyalty-as-a-belief. To be "true to one's principles" is either a metaphor or else an elliptical way of describing loyalty to other men who share those principles and are relying upon you to observe them. With regard to moral commitments to men or institutions, the term "loyalty" is usually reserved for a *total commitment* to the interests, safety, and preservation of the loyalty-object. We can see here one source of the confusion between the concepts of loyalty as a disposition and as a commitment. Speaking loosely, there may be a little difference between a man who lays down his life out of love for his country and another who makes the same sacrifice in fulfillment of his sworn promise of loyalty. When we come to consider the limits of the demands which a state may make upon its subjects, the distinction is quite material indeed.

Within the category of total moral commitment, there are a number of sub-categories which can be distinguished, depending upon the way in which the commitment arises and the person or persons to whom it is made. Some moral obligations are contractual in origin; they come into being through a deliberate, explicit act of commitment, as in a promise or pledge of fealty. Some obligations, on the other hand, are "natural." They have their roots in a human relationship, like that of child to parent, which generates moral commitments without explicit decision. These total commitments, whether natural or contractual in origin, can bind an individual to another person, to a group of persons, or to a social institution conceived as something other than the particular individuals who occupy its ranks at any particular time.*

If we permute and combine the several types of total commitments, we arrive at a convenient classification which displays diagrammatically the relationships among a number of traditional and modern conceptions of political loyalty. The following two-by-three matrix summarizes the six major conceptions of loyalty-as-a-moral-commitment.

OBJECT OF LOYALTY

Type of Obligation	Individual	Group	Institution
Natural	Subject to king; child to parent	Clansman to clan; individual to human race	Native-born to motherland
	Paternal theory of kingship; "family loyalty"	Tribal view of loyalty; World Federalism	Plato's *Crito;* nationalist ideologies
Contractual	Vassal to liege lord	Social Contract	Loyalty oath; naturalization; "implicit contract"
	Medieval theory of feudal king	Locke; Rousseau	Locke; modern legal concept of loyalty

Each box contains examples of a kind of loyalty and authors who have defended such a conception or theories in which it figures. Thus in the middle box of the lower line we

---

* There is an important difference between obligation to an institution and obligation to a group of individuals who may be organized institutionally. This point arises in discussions of social contract theories of political obligation, where the question is whether the original promise of all to all remains in force after some of the original contracting parties have died and others have taken their places.

have an example of contractual total commitment of an individual to a group, namely the social contract, followed by two authors—Locke and Rousseau—who have offered a group-contractual analysis of political loyalty.

1. *Natural Moral Obligation to an Individual:* Under this heading we find the form of authority, and its correlative loyalty, often cited by traditional authors as the prototype of all political authority, namely that of a father over his sons. The obligation of the sons is supposed to stem from the debt they owe their father for having given them existence. The analogy is frequently drawn between the paternal authority of God and that of the head of the family. From extended family to tribe to nation, so Aristotle for example tells us, paternal authority and the duty of filial obedience grow into kingly authority and the subject's duty of loyalty. Although sovereignty has been rationalized and rulers institutionalized, a tendency can still be seen in even the most advanced democracies to invest the political leader with an aura of paternal majesty. Thence comes the horror we feel at the assassination of a Prime Minister or President.

2. *Contractual Moral Obligation to an Individual:* As the tradition of patriarchal tribes gives us the model of natural loyalty to an individual, so the equally ancient institution of the *comitatus* exemplifies contractual loyalty to an individual. In early Germanic culture, it was the practice for an outstanding warrior to gather about him a band of comrades who swore a personal oath to follow him, fight at his side, and lay down their lives for him if necessary. In return they received a share of the booty from the raids which constituted the principal occupation of the group. The custom was fused in early medieval times with Roman practices to form the characteristic feudal relation of vassal to lord. Both parties to the ceremony of fealty were free men, and though the vassal submitted himself to the lord in postures of hu-

mility, he might be, and often was, a count or bishop or even king. In late medieval times, with the growth of mercenary armies and the centralization of political authority, the relationship became more and more an economic contract, and the notion of loyalty to a national king took the place of the old individual fealty.

3. *Natural Moral Obligation to a Group:* The most ancient and the most modern conceptions of loyalty fall into this category. The loyalty of a clansman to his people is one of the earliest moral obligations to be recognized by society. It is based on the ties of kinship, frequently extended and indirect, which unite a tribe into a single "ingroup." The idea has been universalized in the modern concept of loyalty to the whole human race. Opponents of nationalism argue that the same obligation which all men acknowledge to their kinsmen or fellow-citizens is owed by each of us to the human race taken collectively. As with the loyalty of son to father, our obligation to mankind is said to rest on a natural relation, that of a common humanity. In the absence of an adequate analysis of the concept of a collective humanity, it is not clear how we are to distinguish this special debt of loyalty from the general moral obligation to treat all men as ends and take cognizance of their needs and rights.

4. *Contractual Moral Obligation to a Group:* The principal example of this sort of obligation of loyalty is the social contract which, according to political philosophers in the democratic tradition, first creates and defines the political community and gathers together the individual moral authority of the separate individuals into the collective sovereignty of the society. As the name itself implies, the social contract is modeled upon the concept of a legal contract. Several consequences follow from this legal metaphor. First, the parties to the contract are equal before the law, although of course some may be wealthier, more powerful, or of

higher status than others. Second, the contract is a self-interested agreement from which each party expects to gain and under which each party must give. Third, the contract is limited in its scope and force by the terms of the original agreement. Its goals and methods of implementation are more or less explicitly spelled out and there may even be stated circumstances in which the contract is void and the parties have the right to violate it.

5. *Natural Moral Obligation to an Institution:* In the past century and a half political loyalty has by and large been understood as a natural tie binding the individual to his native land. The concept is as old as Socrates, who argues in the *Crito* that he owes a debt of filial obedience to the Athenian Laws which have raised and cared for him. Socrates makes it clear that his obligation is to the laws (i.e., the state) and not to his fellow Athenians. In like manner, many a modern patriot conceives himself as protecting his nation against its present inhabitants and recalling them to its historic faith or mission. In a world which has seen the demystification of authority and the demythologization of Christianity, a religious horror is still felt at the traitor. He is viewed not as a man who has broken a contract or reneged on a debt but as a defiler of sacred things.

6. *Contractual Moral Obligation to an Institution:* As the natural authority of father over son is the original of all political authority, so its most recent variety is the last of our six types, the contractual debt owed to a political institution such as the state. Social contract theory holds that the authority created by the original contract is vested in the state. Thereafter it remains the possession of the state even though the original contracting parties die out and are replaced. New citizens either take a formal oath of allegiance upon admission to the status of citizen or else—as in the case of native-born children who achieve legal maturity—are con-

sidered to have made an implicit contract with the state by remaining in the country and accepting the benefits of citizenship. The voluntary character of contractual political obligation is preserved in most social contract theories by the fiction that the citizen may leave the country and annul his contract if he is no longer able to support his government in good conscience. There may just barely have been some reality in this notion in the seventeenth century, when Locke advanced it. Today, with the earth's surface exhaustively divided into sovereign nations, not even the wealthy man can escape submission to some state or other. The only sizable group of people in the modern world who owe no political allegiance are the displaced persons and refugees who live a life of bare subsistence and wait for a chance to return to their native land.

II

We have now distinguished four distinct senses of the term "loyal," and six sub-categories of the fourth sense. One might think that was more than enough conceptual machinery for analyzing the problem of political loyalty, but there are still two more distinctions which need to be drawn before we can discuss the subject with any measure of clarity. In a way, the elaborateness of the analytical tools which we need for the job is a measure of its difficulty, and an indication of the tangle of confusions which we can stumble into if we simply plunge right into an argument over loyalty oaths and security boards.

The first distinction is between two different senses of the term "disloyal." It is, after all, disloyalty rather than loyalty which causes all the disagreement. Now, disloyalty is, of course, the opposite or negative of loyalty, so we might simply match off every sense of loyalty with its corresponding opposite. But there are *two* different kinds of opposites, which logicians identify by the labels "contradictory" and "contrary." The contradictory of a term is simply its denial or negation. For example, the contradictory of black is not-black; the contradictory of strong is not-strong. When we deny the application of a term to some entity, we make no positive assertion about the character, or even the existence, of that thing. The contrary of a term, on the other hand, is another independent term which we imagine to stand in some opposed relation to it. The contrary of black is *white*, the contrary of strong is *weak*. A pair of contrary terms can be conceived as lying at opposite ends of a continuum defined by the presence or absence of some property. The ancients, for example, thought that white and black lay at the ends of the spectrum according to whether color was present or absent. The several colors were thought to be aligned between the two extremes.

"Disloyalty" can be taken either as the contradictory or as the contrary of "loyalty." Disloyalty as the contradictory would be simply the denial of loyalty. Disloyalty, understood as the contrary of loyalty, would be a character trait, legal status, belief, or moral condition, in some sense opposite to loyalty. There would presumably be a middle ground which was defined neither as loyalty nor as disloyalty. The point appears quibbling, but it has far-reaching consequences. There is all the difference in the world between a government which demands that its citizens be loyal in the sense of simply not being disloyal, and a government which requires active, positive displays of adherence to official dogmas and support for official positions. The difference is expressed by the two sayings, "Everyone who is not against us is with us!" and "Anyone who is not with us is against us!"

The notion of positive loyalty has about it the flavor of coerced belief that we associate with totalitarian regimes, but democratic nations have also been known to demand from their citizens more than merely the absence of positive disloyalty. For example, the Supreme Court decisions concerning a mandatory flag salute in public schools turn on the issue of the state's right to require positive displays (presumably sincere) of loyalty to the United States. In the peculiar circumstances of American life, this issue has become tangled with the quite distinct debate over religious liberty, and the Court has tended to release schoolchildren from the obligation of saluting when a conflicting religious or quasi-religious belief is involved. Nevertheless, whenever the political temperature of the nation rises a few degrees and enemies, foreign and domestic, are descried, the demands go out for displays of positive loyalty, and any hesitation to comply is taken as evidence of disloyalty. The indecent eagerness of so many American liberals to garnish their timid dissent with anticommunist protestations is an evidence of their perpetual fear of accusations of insufficient loyalty.

To each sense of "loyal" we can attach both a contradictory and a contrary sense of "disloyal." Thus, if loyalty is conceived as a character trait, then disloyalty will be either the mere lack of that trait (contradictory) or some distinct and opposite trait disposing the individual to betray his nation, fail to come to its defense, and so forth (contrary). Loyalty as a legal status has as its opposites the lack of that status (contradictory) or another status, like that of criminal, carrying various penalties and determined by law (contrary). In the case of loyalty as a belief, disloyalty is either absence of the belief (contradictory) or a conflicting belief (contrary). The analogy in religion is agnosticism versus atheism. Finally, if loyalty is interpreted as the honoring of a total commitment, then disloyalty is either the mere failure to keep the commitment or else the deliberate breach of it for some conflicting purpose, not necessarily self-regarding.

The second distinction we need is that between actual and potential loyalty or disloyalty. The concept of potential loyalty is rather complex, and it will help to consider it in connection with each of our four senses of loyalty in turn.

1. If loyalty is a character trait, then it is already in a certain sense a potentiality. Courage is the disposition, or potentiality, to act bravely when faced with danger. As Aristotle pointed out, a man may be potentially courageous either in the sense that he now has the disposition to act bravely, or in the sense that he has the capacity to develop that disposition. Analogously, a child is said to have musical talent, meaning that he has it within him to become a fine musician; an accomplished musician, by contrast, is said to be a fine pianist, meaning that although he is not now performing, he can do so (actualize his potentiality) when he chooses. As I mentioned in my discussion of loyalty as a character trait, one analysis of such traits makes the performance of some characteristic acts or other a necessary condition of having the trait, while a second analysis does not. The former will apply the concept of potential loyalty to persons who have not yet given evidence of their loyal disposition; the latter will employ the concept of actual loyalty rather more widely.

There is a certain asymmetry in the interpretation of the concept of disloyalty by the loyalty-as-character-trait school. Whereas a man is said to be loyal insofar as he is disposed to act in defense of his nation, etc., he is often said to be disloyal only when he has actually committed a breach of faith. In that sense, "loyalty" is what Gilbert Ryle has called a disposition-term, and disloyalty is what he calls an occurrence-term. Nevertheless, one can find some instances in which a man's loyalty is questioned not because he has committed some act, but because he is likely to do so. A man might be called chronically disloyal, despite the fact that he has not in the present instance broken faith, because he is thought to be prone to disloyalty. This, indeed, is one of the grounds on which alcoholics and homosexuals were denied security clearance by the State Department.

2. Strictly speaking, there is no valid use of the concept of potential loyalty in the case of loyalty-as-a-legal-status. Either a man has the status of citizen in good standing or he has not. We may of course predict the outcome of a loyalty hearing, just as we may predict the outcome of a murder trial, but the injunction to treat a man as innocent until proven guilty holds good in all cases of ascription of legal status. It may be reasonable to bar a man from government employ because he is thought likely to commit acts which would ordinarily be punished by a judgment of disloyalty. However, if disloyalty is a legal status, then a man is not disloyal until he has been so judged by an appropriate tribunal.

3. The distinction between actual and potential loyalty has an equally dubious application in the case of loyalty-as-a-belief. One could think up some meaning for the term "potential belief," but in general it hardly seems a useful concept to define. One might imagine cases, for example, in which a religious or political leader, alert to the dangers of heresy in his flock, came to recognize certain types as prone to heterodoxy. He could then say of someone, "He is one of the faithful at present, but his sort is prone to fall away, he is potentially unfaithful."

4. Moral commitments are in some respects like character traits, in that a man may correctly be said to have and honor a moral commitment even when, at the moment, he is doing nothing which relates to it in any way. If I have sworn to defend my country in time of war, and if I remain so resolved, then I am a loyal citizen even though my country is at peace and I am quietly minding my business. To acknowledge and honor a commitment is to do what is re-

quired by the commitment when the occasion arises. Save in odd cases like keeping a secret, where not doing something moment by moment is what is required, moral commitments are operative only intermittently. It would be absurd to say that between wars, the valiant soldier is not loyal because he is not then fighting.

We encounter once again the asymmetry in the concepts of loyalty and disloyalty which appeared in the case of loyalty-as-a-character-trait. When a man is called "loyal" it is never meant simply that he has committed certain acts, although those acts may be evidence of his loyalty. Whether loyalty is conceived as a character trait, a legal status, a belief, or the fulfillment of an obligation, it is something more than any number of specific acts. (Namely, a proneness to commit acts of that sort, or a legal status ascribed because of those acts, or a belief which issues in acts like those, or a moral commitment which those acts serve to honor.) Disloyalty, however, is sometimes treated not as a proneness to certain acts, or as a legal status ascribed because of certain acts, etc., but simply as the performance of those acts themselves. In part this follows from the fact that a single counter-instance refutes a universal judgment. Hence, if "disloyal" simply means "not loyal," any disloyal act is enough to destroy the implied universality of "He is (unfailingly) loyal." In part, however, it is a reflection of the fact that whereas "loyal" is most often taken to mean "having the character trait of loyalty" or "honoring a total commitment," the contrary term "disloyal" usually has the legalistic sense of having broken some law or security regulation.

III

We come finally to the substantive question which lies at the heart of all disputes about loyalty, the question which might be said to encompass the entire philosophy of politics: Does a state ever have the right to demand the loyalty of its subjects? Or, to turn the question around and state it in a way which focuses on the individual, Does a man ever have a moral obligation to be loyal to the state? The great medieval debates about the origin and location of sovereignty, the modern disputes over the rights and limits of civil disobedience, all come together in this simple question.

In the light of the analysis which we have just completed, it might seem that the obvious answer is, "It depends on what you mean by loyalty." Indeed, this is the right answer, as we shall see. But I should like to try to narrow the issue somewhat by performing a preliminary application of the results of our analysis of loyalty. Instead of proceeding directly to the question, Does an individual owe loyalty to the state, let us first ask, In what senses of the term "loyalty" would it even be *possible* for a state to require that its subjects be loyal?

This move, from actuality to possibility as it were, is a typical philosophical maneuver. Perhaps I can make it a bit clearer by an analogy. Suppose that we wanted to know whether scientists could construct a thinking machine. The first step, obviously, would be to analyze the term "thinking." Once we had identified a number of distinct meanings associated with the term, we might ask, in connection with each one of them, whether in *that* sense of "thinking" it was even logically possible for scientists to build a thinking machine. For example, one meaning of "thinking" might be "assembling information and solving problems." Presumably, there is no logical impossibility about a machine that could do that. But another meaning might be "activity of an immaterial soul." Obviously a scientist cannot build an immaterial soul. Hence, we can say a priori that *if* thinking means the activity of an immaterial soul, *then* scientists cannot build a thinking machine.

Now let us look at the four senses of loyalty already distinguished and in each case try to decide whether it is even possible for a government to demand loyalty, in that sense, from its subjects.

If we understand loyalty as a character trait, then the state clearly never has the right to demand that its subjects be loyal. The first principle of all moral philosophy is that a man cannot have an obligation to do what it is not within his power to do. It makes no more sense to demand that a man have a loyal disposition toward the state than it would to require that he be naturally courageous or possess a generous temperament. The state might demand certain *acts* of loyalty, or the forebearance from certain acts of disloyalty, for acts *are* within our power to do or abstain. But a man simply cannot, by an act of will, alter his personality.

The local, state, and federal governments in the United States do not require loyal dispositions from their citizens (though a number of enthusiastic legislators are perpetually engaged in attempts to write such demands into law). But they *do* require American citizens to take part in activities whose purpose is to create and sustain such dispositions. The public schools not only teach romantic versions of American history in an effort to inspire pupils with a love for their country; they also require regular ritual repetitions of ceremonial gestures and incantations which are thought to be particularly efficacious in producing a disposition of loyalty. Justice Frankfurter, in a famous Supreme Court decision (Minersville School District v. Gobitis), defended the right of the state to require such rituals in the following words:

> The ultimate foundation of a free society is the binding tie of cohesive sentiment. Such a sentiment is fostered by all those agencies of the mind and spirit which may serve to gather up the traditions of a people, transmit

them from generation to generation, and thereby create
that continuity of a treasured common life which constitutes a civilization. . . . The influences which help toward a common feeling for the common country are
manifold. Some may seem harsh and others no doubt
foolish. Surely, however, the end is legitimate.

We may question the moral legitimacy of patriotic education, however much we grant its logical possibility. For
myself, I see too close a similarity between such education
and the totalitarian indoctrination of other nations. Nevertheless, one thing is clear; no state has the right to demand
success in its efforts at inspiring loyalty. Just as it makes no
sense to require an adult to love his country, so we cannot
in reason compel a child to develop such a sentiment, no
matter how many rituals we impose upon him.

In sum, if loyalty is understood as a personality trait,
then no state ever has the right to demand loyalty of its
citizens, even if it does have the right to submit them to
patriotic education.

Beliefs, like traits of character, cannot be commanded.
If being loyal to a nation-state means believing in some
political ideology which it is supposed to embody, then no
state ever has the right to command its subjects to be loyal.
It may perhaps require them to utter ritual words ("I
pledge allegiance . . .") or to sign oaths promising never to
falter in the faith, but the significance of such acts will be
nil. So long as a man retains coherent autonomy of his
cognitive faculties—so long, that is, as he is not brainwashed
—he cannot be forced to believe. The essence of belief is its
free origin in the rational processes of the mind. We can no
more force a free man to believe in democracy by making
him pledge allegiance than we can make a fundamentalist
believe in evolution by requiring him to read aloud *The
Origin of Species.*

The interpretation of loyalty as orthodoxy leads quite naturally to censorship, inquisitions, and all the hated concomitances of an established religious or political dogma. For that reason, one might expect men of a liberal persuasion to avoid such an interpretation and fix instead on one of the other possibilities. Nevertheless, when the question arose of the right of communists to teach in schools and universities, a great many liberals argued that in order to be granted such a right, a man must "accept the ground rules of free debate on which a liberal society is founded." Put somewhat less circumspectly, communists were to confess their faith in Mill's *On Liberty* before being admitted to the classroom. Those who found themselves in all honesty unable to subscribe to the liberal creed were to be academically excommunicated.

Now, of course, the liberals didn't view the matter in this light at all. To them it would have appeared grotesque to use words like "confess" and "faith" and "excommunicate" to describe their position. Indeed, they couldn't see that communists were being forced to believe anything substantive at all; the only requirement was acceptance of a purely formal or procedural rule for the regulation of debate. Only close-minded ideologues or sinister hypocrites could reject the principles of the free marketplace of ideas!

Since the first chapter of this book is devoted to refuting precisely those principles, I shall not comment upon them here, save to remark that true believers always find it impossible to imagine that decent men could honestly disagree with them. If a member of the intellectual community is permitted to question every dogma save the dogma on which that community organizes itself, then he is no freer than a Chinese professor forced to chant the sayings of Mao. There is, of course, an alternative. Following the wise and forgiving practice of the Roman Catholic Church, liberals could announce themselves willing to gather to their bosoms all those souls who, though unable to believe, nevertheless submitted themselves to the superior authority of John Stuart Mill. As usual, we could expect that there would be more rejoicing in academia over the return of one sinner than . . .

What shall we say of loyalty considered as the honoring of a total moral commitment? In this case it would seem that we can readily make sense of the state's demand that its subjects be loyal. If the moral commitment is conceived as a natural obligation, then the government would, like the Laws in Plato's dialogue *The Crito,* demand that the citizen acknowledge the debt he had incurred to the state by living within its territory, accepting its protection, and benefiting from its institutions. In the case of loyalty-as-a-contractual-obligation, the state would either remind the citizen of the agreement he had made, or appeal to the concept of an implicit contract to prove that every adult citizen had made a quasi-contract with the state.

The essence of a moral commitment is that it be freely made. In political terms, this means that the citizens have an alternative to binding themselves to the state, namely emigration. Most social contract theorists include an emigration clause in order to make sense of the notion of an implicit contract. The theory of contracts in law posits two free and legally equal parties who come together in agreement for mutual benefit. If one of the parties has no choice in the matter—if there is coercion—then the contract is not binding. The analogous argument is presupposed in political theories. In the modern world emigration is in general impossible. The question inevitably arises, therefore, whether a state can have the right to demand a total moral commitment from what is essentially a captive citizenry. I am not asking here whether it is wise or just for the state to make such a demand but only whether it makes sense for it to do so. The answer clearly is that when an individual has no choice in the matter, it is illogical to ask him to choose. Hence, insofar as loyalty is viewed as a total moral commitment of the citizen to the state (or of the citizen to his fellow-citizens), the state cannot have even the possibility of a right to demand that commitment save in the most special of circumstances which rarely exist in the modern world.

There remains only the conception of loyalty as the legal status of full citizenship. Clearly the state by its very nature has a right to demand such "loyalty" from its citizens, for that is simply to demand that they *be* citizens. Attention in this case shifts to the criteria which are laid down by the state for citizenship, but whatever they are, the method of ascertaining "loyalty" will be hedged round with all the safeguards adumbrated by the phrase "due process."

Obviously there can be no justification for a legal definition of citizenship which makes reference to or requires character traits or beliefs. Nor can a moral commitment be demanded as a precondition of citizenship, save perhaps in the unusual case of immigrants who theoretically have an alternative to residence in the United States. The appropriate sorts of criteria, I would suggest, are the familiar qualifications of birthplace, parentage, and residence, together with the absence of any defeating facts such as conflicting citizenship, past convictions for specified crimes, and so forth. Loyalty thus conceived is purely a function of behavior; it does not involve the inner man, neither his beliefs nor his inclinations and character. It also does not place him in the false position of having to announce a moral commitment as though he had freely chosen it when in fact it has been forced upon him.

It should now be clear that the United States has no

right to demand any sort of loyalty of its citizens which goes beyond merely fulfilling the legal conditions for ordinary citizenship. In a voluntary community which men could join or leave at will, different and more stringent conditions might reasonably be imposed, but we are too far from the world imagined by Locke and Rousseau to invoke their ideal of a social contract.

In light of these conclusions, we might expect American liberals to shun the interpretation of loyalty as a character trait or orthodoxy, and instead restrict themselves to the notion of legal citizenship. Their widespread emotional rejection of oaths, affidavits, and investigations of personal behavior confirms that expectation. Nevertheless, when American social scientists of a liberal political persuasion turn their professional attentions to the subject of loyalty, they surprisingly embrace a sociological rather than a legal interpretation. This tendency, which I have already remarked as a universal characteristic of contemporary liberal thought, is clearly displayed in *The Loyal and the Disloyal* by Morton Grodzins, which appeared in 1956. Professor Grodzins, a Chicago political scientist who had published a study of the effect of internment on Japanese-Americans during World War II, broadened his investigations to produce a systematic theory of political loyalty. Grodzins' aim was to base topical political commentary on social scientific foundations. He interpreted loyalty essentially as a personality trait fostered and sustained by certain social relationships and institutional settings.

Grodzins conceives of loyalties as habit patterns which organize and orient human interrelationships. As such, they are indispensable elements in the formation and maintenance of personality. "It is a contradiction in terms to speak of a man without loyalties. He does not exist." (p. 5) Loyalties are "given in return for gratifications received. They organize the life of the individual, reducing the area of his uncertainty and anxiety. . . . One is loyal to the groups that provide gratifications because what serves the group serves the self; what threatens the group threatens the self. There is no self outside group activity." (p. 6)

Loyalty on this view is in the first instance an attitude of identification of self with some primary group of persons from whom one seeks gratifications, either material or psychological. The principal gratification, perhaps, is simply the confirmation of one's own self-image which is provided by the expected responses of the group. Loyalty to the state, Grodzins argues, is built up out of the interlocking and pyramiding of loyalties to primary and intermediate groups. The state is thus only indirectly an object of loyalty, and as Grodzins makes clear, it may be an ambiguous object when the several primary loyalties of an individual's life fail to integrate and pyramid completely. Thus a German-American feels a conflict of loyalties in 1940 because his identification with the culture and society of Germany cannot be integrated with his identification with his American neighborhood, church, or place of business. So too, a scientist experiences a contradiction between his loyalty to the international community of physicists, which includes Soviet and Chinese scientists, and his loyalty to home and society as symbolized in the security regulations of the American government.

Grodzins' intentions are "liberal." That is to say, he deploys his psychology of loyalty for the purpose of eliciting sympathy for Japanese-Americans torn between their native and adopted lands; he speaks with sweet reasonableness to the red-hunters of the loyalty-security program. The following is a characteristic passage:

> Those responsible for security should recognize that loyalties change with time and circumstance. They should

recognize that affiliations of the past are less important than actions of the present. They should recognize that investigation can erode loyalty as well as disclose disloyalty. They should recognize that men properly have multiple loyalties in a democratic state, that superpatriotism is not always a desirable attribute, and that judgments concerning security are more limited and easier to make than those concerning loyalty. They should recognize that all men have a disloyalty (and loyalty) potential, that some risk is therefore inevitable in all government enterprise, and that [as Alan Barth has said] absolute security is likely to result in nothing save absolute sterility.

In short, Grodzins endorses the government's demand that its citizens exhibit an emotional identification with the United States, but he cautions against stupid, narrow, self-defeating methods of ascertaining whether that character trait is present in government employees. When he writes that affiliations of the past are less important than actions of the present, he does not mean that men's loyalty should not be judged by their affiliations; he merely means that such affiliations are usually less significant evidence than are present actions (including *present* affiliations, presumably). If I may draw an irreverent (but not, I think, irrelevant) analogy, Grodzins' relation to the red-hunters is rather like that of the Jesuits to the Jansenists. Like so many other liberals, he objects to the loyalty and security program because it was conducted by insensitive bigots who used its machinery as a device for proscribing all manner of behavior and belief that they feared or disliked. In short, Grodzins' criticism is that the program was carried out *inefficiently*. There is no disagreement about its ends, or about its conception of loyalty.

The liberal confusion concerning the nature of loyalty is perfectly epitomized by the heated debate over the notion of guilt by association. During the height of the loyalty crisis, many an individual's loyalty was called into question because he was friendly with a member of the Communist party, had been part of a social circle of people with left-wing politics, was the son or father or brother of a suspicious person, or even because he liked the ballet and subscribed to foreign (noncommunist) publications. There was a great deal of know-nothing parochial stupidity in the administration of the loyalty program, as many of the more sophisticated red-hunters themselves complained. It was therefore dangerously easy for at least some liberals to concentrate their attacks on instances of crudity or ignorance and so avoid a direct confrontation with the principles which underlay the program. It was outrageous to brand a man disloyal because of the friends he made and the journals he read. And yet, the spy trials revealed that a distressingly high proportion of those convicted were intellectuals, former adherents of left-wing causes, friends or relations of Communists, and even readers of foreign publications. Liberals found themselves in the impossible position of maintaining that who a man knew and what he read would give no clue to his political convictions or probable future behavior.

If loyalty is indeed a character trait, then nothing could be more relevant to its discovery than associations, interests, and kinship ties. Here, for example, is an account of the way loyalties are formed, written by another liberal student of the problem of loyalty, Professor John Schaar:

> What is called loyalty is really a kind of norm . . . resting upon the familiar processes of attitude formation and change. The roots of loyalty are to be found in social interaction. Expressed briefly, shared activities evoke shared activities of sympathy. As the group lives together as a social unit, members experience mutual debts of gratitude, mutual likes and dislikes, and shared

interests which bind them together. This culminates in
the simply stated and profoundly felt emotion of owing
much to each other and to the group as a whole.*

In short, associations are the very source of loyalty-as-a-
character-trait. They are not merely legitimate evidence
of loyalty, they are the *primary* evidence of it. "Where
there's smoke, there's fire," may be a bad rule of law, but it
is the first principle of social psychology! A man's personal
and political associations are perfectly good empirical evidence for his inclinations and attitudes. Indeed, used intelligently and with a certain sophistication, even information
about his tastes in art and literature are *some* indication
about his political attitudes and probable behavior!

It is instructive to compare liberals' criticisms of the
loyalty investigations with their attacks, during the same
years, on the foreign policy of Dulles and Eisenhower. A
great deal was made of Dulles' moralizing (again the Jesuit-
Jansenist contrast), Eisenhower's lack of intellectual graces,
and the embarrassing failure of new ambassadors to remember the names of the prime ministers of the countries to
which they were assigned. This critique of technique was
put forward as fundamental analysis of policy, with the expectation that all our state department needed was to promote career officers to ambassadorial posts, learn some foreign languages, and act a bit less like fundamentalists loose
in the big city. John F. Kennedy was greeted by liberals as
the answer to their prayers. He was young, bright, atten-
tive to academic advice, had actually written a book, and
was married to a woman who spoke fluent French. Consequently, it came as something of a shock when this paragon
of liberal virtues invaded Cuba and brought the world to
the brink of a nuclear war. In the aftermath of the Cuban

* Loyalty in America, 1957, p. 16.

adventure, liberal ranks split into two unequal groups. The majority, confronted by the refutation of their confident faith that technique was all that American foreign policy had lacked, retreated into the brittle cold-war belligerence of the Roches and Rostows. The remainder were forced into an examination of the roots of American policy in an effort to discover where it had gone wrong. This radical turn of the American left was of course considerably aided by the death of Kennedy. Yet so susceptible is the ordinary American liberal to beguiling personalities and the superficies of sophistication that many who were disenchanted with John Kennedy had already begun to reenchant themselves with Robert Kennedy.

Finally, let us give some consideration to the "loyalty oath" which has played so prominent a role in American political debates. There are two distinct sorts of depositions which are both somewhat confusedly referred to as "loyalty oaths." The first, the loyalty oath proper, is a pledge to uphold the Constitution of the United States (or of one of the fifty states) and protect it from its enemies "both foreign and domestic." The second is an affidavit swearing to certain matters of fact, such as that one is not now and never has been a member of the Communist party, or that one is not a member of some other organization proscribed by the federal government. The affidavit is quite clearly a dubious legal instrument. If the activities to which it refers are against the law, then it invades the constitutional protection against self-incrimination; if the activities are legal, then the affidavit is a method of punishing an individual nonjudicially. In practice the affidavit is an unsavory device for transforming a legal act into an illegal one. A man is asked to swear that he has not done X, an act which is perfectly legal. He knows that if he refuses to swear, he will suffer the loss of a job, social and professional ostracism, and other quasi-punishments. If he lies to avoid those sanctions, he can then be prosecuted for perjury, even though not for the original act. All in all, not a pretty business.

The loyalty oath is quite another matter. If the state is conceived to be founded upon a social contract, then the original promise of each to all *is* a loyalty oath. It is a pledge to accept the decisions of the duly constituted government as one's own, to make such sacrifices for the good of all as may be demanded, and to defend the political community against its enemies. Thus, if loyalty is interpreted as the honoring of a contractual total commitment, then every citizen is assumed to have taken an oath of loyalty and to be bound by its conditions. It may be doubted whether anything is gained from constant reiterations of the pledge, but no social contract theorist could ever deny the government's right to require it.

The matter is rather different once we acknowledge the inapplicability of the social contract model to contemporary politics. When a man has no real choice but to live in the country of his birth, the demand that he swear loyalty to it has the quality of a coerced promise which is morally worthless. States can perhaps require their subjects to obey the laws and punish them for not doing so. But it makes no sense, in addition, for the government to exact the lip service of a loyalty oath.

Loyalty oaths are inappropriate as well in the cases of loyalty-as-a-character-trait and loyalty-as-a-belief. In the former, a willingness to take the oath may be one sign of a loyal disposition, but since one cannot acquire a new personality trait by an act of will, the oath is not morally binding. As for loyalty-as-a-belief, the appropriate instrument would be a confession of faith or catechism rather than an oath of loyalty.

3. Power

THE QUESTION which most sharply divides radicals from liberals in modern America is well expressed in the title of Robert Dahl's influential study of New Haven politics: *Who Governs?* The traditional liberal view, from the eighteenth-century notion of separation of powers to Galbraith's modern theory of countervailing powers, has been that power in the United States is diffused and scattered among a plurality of competing interests and elites so that no single group acquires a monopoly of control, and no significant segment of the population is entirely excluded from the exercise of political power. By contrast, the common theme of radical critics is the existence of a concentration of power in the hands of a class or interlocking set of factions whose will is imposed on the people behind a facade of ineffectual democratic institutions. C. Wright Mills crystallized the radical theory for American readers with his enormously influential book, *The Power Elite*. Since then, the English term "Establishment" has been adopted to describe the supposed domination of American life by a system of private and public institutions whose governors shuttle from executive suite to executive suite in a closed circle from which the great mass of ordinary Americans are quite thoroughly excluded. Recently, the term "Power Structure" has been taken over by the more militant leaders of the Negro movement as a label for the white leaders who block escape from the ghetto and control the jobs and homes for which the slum dweller reaches out.

It would be easy to interpret this apparent opposition of views as merely a rhetorical war of words growing out of differing emphases on essentially the same picture of American life. The liberals, after all, are quite well aware that political power is unevenly distributed among American citizens; and radicals, when pressed, will acknowledge that there is no cabal or conscious conspiracy manipulating a docile public. Perhaps we have here no more than a difference of temperament: liberals tend to emphasize the stability of the American political system and its responsiveness to pressures from aroused citizens; radicals are enraged by the misery and injustice which flourish in the midst of such wealth, and refuse to relax into attitudes of self-congratulation when confronted by so great a gulf between what is and what could be.

Such a resolution of the disagreement would be easy, but it would also be wrong. Behind the rhetoric lies a genuine dispute, not so much over the actual nature of American politics, but rather over the norms or standards by which a modern political society should be judged. To be sure, the issue is hopelessly confused by the conceptual imprecision with which it is debated, but the instincts of the participants are accurate. Radicals and liberals really do go separate ways over the question of political power. If we are to evaluate the soundness of modern liberal philosophy, we must attempt to come to grips with the concept of power.

I

Instead of launching a frontal attack on the concept of power, let us approach the subject obliquely by explicating the notion of an "object of decision." By an object of decision I mean any event or state of affairs which someone or other is in a position actually to choose to bring about. For example, I can if I choose walk from my study to my kitchen and pour myself a glass of beer. Therefore, my having a beer is *an object of my decision.* Similarly, I can if I choose buy a car, although it will strain my resources to do so. So my buying a car is also an object of my decision. On the other hand, I cannot as things now stand choose to run a mile in four minutes or play the Beethoven violin concerto flawlessly. Therefore those things are not objects of my decision.

There is virtually no state of affairs or event which is an object of decision for every single person, although there are countless things which are objects of no one's decision at all. For example, no one at the moment has it within his ability to choose to vacation on the moon, while some unfortunate people cannot even choose to take a breath or open their eyes. Obviously also there are many things which groups of people can choose to do as groups, but which no single individual can choose to do. Some of these, like playing a game of baseball or having a discussion, logically require several people for their accomplishment. Others, like lifting a truck, simply happen as a matter of fact to require the cooperation of a number of individuals.

In addition, there are some things which are not actually within a given individual's scope of choice, despite the fact that he is legally authorized to choose them and his right to do so is acknowledged by everyone around him. It is a commonplace of American politics, for example, that the powers which the Constitution and laws give to the President are far in excess of his real ability to translate his will into practice. Every new incumbent discovers the mysterious capacity of even the most precise directives to disappear without trace into the innards of the State Department. Robert McNamara earned himself a permanent place in history merely by exercising in fact a measure of the authority which every previous Secretary of Defense had exercised only in theory.

Many of the unclarities and ambiguities which becloud the notion of power are present as well in the notion of an object of decision. If the only advantage enjoyed by Secretary McNamara over his predecessors was his superior administrative skill, should we say that effective management of the Department of Defense was, or was not, a real object of their choice? To take another example, if I can bring about some state of affairs only by employing means which, for some reason or other, I consider unacceptable, is that state of affairs an object of my decision or not? A complete analysis of the concept of power would require that these ambiguities be diminished, but for our purposes it will be possible to put them to one side and develop other implications of the notion of an object of decision.

Of particular importance is the case of the event or state of affairs which is a *consequence* of decisions, but yet is not itself an *object* of decision. This is the "unintended consequence" which economists and sociological theorists have made so much of in their analyses of large-scale social behavior. A traffic jam, for example, is the consequence of thousands of individual decisions by motorists—decisions to visit the kids, to go to the store, to take in a movie, to get out of town. As a result of all those decisions, too many cars arrive simultaneously at a bridge or tunnel or inter-section which can't handle the load. *But no one at all de-cided to cause a traffic jam.* Hence the traffic jam is not properly an object of anyone's decision.

Social life is full of occurrences and situations which are *consequences* of individual or collective decisions but are not *objects* of decision. In the early days of liberal optimism, social philosophers tended to call attention to the felicitous consequences which issued unintended from the interplay of unconnected decisions. Adam Smith's famous image of the "invisible hand" captured the liberal confidence that the public good would unintentionally but efficiently be served by countless self-interested decisions in the daily economic activities of a free market. Latterly, sociologists of a liberal political bent have been influenced by the pessi-mism of the conservative continental sociological tradition, so that today the phrase "unintended consequences" does indeed conjure up traffic jams rather than prosperity. One of the characteristic arguments of piecemeal social reformers against the more systematic proposals of their opponents to the left is the impossibility of forestalling the unfortunate and unintended byproducts of even the best-intentioned programs. Naturally, conservatives view even piecemeal re-forms with apprehension. They are fond of invoking the metaphor of society as an organism in an attempt to dis-suade liberal tinkerers from upsetting the delicate equilib-rium of social life.

In addition to the notion of an object of decision, we shall have need of a distinction, admittedly vague, between matters of little or no social importance and matters of major social importance. The daily actions of an ordinary citizen are not, save under the most unusual of circumstances, matters of major social importance, but the actions of the President are. Among matters which are currently objects of someone's decision, the level of federal taxation is of major importance while the marital life of the President's daughter is not (though it may, of course, be a matter of major public curiosity). The distinction is patently imprecise, and I do not wish to pretend by the elaboration of technical jargon that it can be made much more precise. Nevertheless, I shall persist in employing it because, as we shall see presently, it is indispensable to an analysis of the concept of political power.

It might be worth pointing out that the notion of a matter of major social importance, in addition to being imprecise, is also relative to the values and interests of the members of the society. In the United States, for example, virtually everything related to the overall size and distribution of the gross national product qualifies as a matter of major social importance, but in a devoutly religious society which cared little for material wealth, signs of divine favor or disfavor might far outweigh in importance mere fluctuations in production. Some of the most intractable social disputes concern the relative ranking of different matters rather than the choosing of a course of action with regard to any one of them.

Any adequate analysis of the distribution of political power in American society would require an investigation of the sorts of matters of major social importance which are, and are not, objects of someone's decision. There are, after all, two questions which can always be asked about any event or state of affairs: First, is it an object of anyone's decision at all? and Second, who decides it? I suggest that *which* matters are objects of someone's decision in a society is a more significant fact about that society than *who* decides them. Hence, modern Russia strikes us as more like modern America than either society is like its eighteenth-century counterpart.

Indeed, there is something like a law of historical development—one of the very few—to the effect that once a matter of major social importance becomes an object of decision, it never reverts to the status of fact of nature or unintended consequence. This might also be called the law of the progress of rationality, for there is a fundamental sense of the term "rational" in which "to be rational" means "to be the author of one's actions, to act rather than to be acted upon." To become *more* rational, in this root sense, means to transform into ends things which previously were not ends. A man becomes more rational just insofar as he brings within the scope of his will some datum of experience which previously confronted him as independent of his will.*

Once any feature of the social world is known to be within human control, it is irrevocably an object of decision, so that even the failure to act with regard to it becomes a deliberate decision. For example, so long as a government is ignorant of the technique of controlling the volume of money in the economy, it must view that fact of social life

* Liberals, by and large, employ only the more superficial notion of rationality as the fitting of means to ends. In this sense of the term, rationality is equivalent to efficiency. Ends or goals are viewed as given by feeling, and hence not open to rational deliberation. From this identification of goals with feelings and means with reason, it is not a very long step to the much-celebrated value neutrality with which modern liberal social scientists emasculate their research. They are unable, for example, to see that a society which fails even to set itself certain social goals—which fails, that is, to make certain matters of importance objects of collective decision—is to that extent an *irrational* society. Naturally, since they cannot see this fact, they cannot undertake as social scientists to explain it. Hence, they remain at the level of predicting variations in public preferences among toothpastes or presidential candidates.

as on a par with the weather. But once it learns the trick of expanding or contracting bank loans, the volume of money is ever after an object of decision, whether it chooses to avail itself of its ability or not. The willingness to recognize this fact, as we shall see, distinguishes political conservatives from political reactionaries.

Irreversible historical progress, as opposed merely to historical alteration, takes place when some matter of major social importance first becomes an object of someone's decision within the society. The most striking series of such extensions of rational decision is to be found in the area of economic activity. Initially, men find themselves engaged in production and exchange. Gradually, they become aware of apparently objective laws governing the relations of prices, wages, profits, and interest levels in the market. What seem to them at first to be iron laws, as foolish to flout as the laws of physics, slowly are recognized as possible objects of collective decision. The total production of goods and services in a society—its Gross National Product—is of course a *consequence* of the economic decisions of acts in the market, but it can also itself be an *object* of social decision. Even so abstract a fact as the annual rate of growth of the GNP may become a direct object of deliberate decision. As knowledge grows and modes of collective action are devised, there is a steady expansion of the realm of decision. So in the history of society the conception of babies is first an inexplicable accident, then an uncontrollable outcome of natural human activities, then a planned event, and finally a part of a national policy regulating the birthrate.

Eventually, through a generalization from social experience, the general concept of a social problem may be formulated. There is a natural series of stages through which each problem progresses. First the problem is identified. In some cases, the recognition of a problem may require nothing more than a deep breath of polluted city air or a brief ride through ghetto slums. In other cases, however, only refined techniques of statistical analysis will reveal the existence of the problem, as when comparisons are made of rates of unemployment among Negro and white workers, or when infant mortality rates in the United States and Scandinavia are contrasted. Next, the causal determinants of the phenomena under examination are discovered. Finally, ways are found to make the phenomena objects of social decision. At this point, what was initially a fact of society has become a subject of policy deliberation. Once such a transformation has been achieved, there is no going back. The age of social innocence is lost, and from that moment any decision, including the decision to do nothing, is a deliberate policy for which the authors of the decision can be held responsible.

At any point in the history of a society, there will be a body of matters of major social importance which are clearly objects of someone's decision, and a number of not-yet-determinate matters which are for the first time being brought within the sphere of rational choice. A conservative, generally speaking, is a man who resists bringing new matters of importance within the scope of decision. For reasons either of tradition or of timidity, or from a frequently well-grounded fear of the loss of social innocence, he prefers to see even quite important matters left to the interplay of individual decisions. To the conservative, unintended consequences are preferable to deliberate decisions. The reactionary, on the other hand, is a man who indulges in the fantasy of returning to a time of innocence before some matter of social importance became an object of decision. He literally wishes to turn the clock back, and of course he is doomed to perpetual disappointment. Before the development of modern economic theory, governments were unable to control the cycle of booms and busts which dominated nineteenth-century Europe and America. Now that we know how to dampen the fluctuations, we can, as a deliberate policy, choose to allow the full swing of inflation and depression, but we can never return to the time when the GNP was an uncontrollable fact of nature.

We sympathize with the reactionary, of course. It is pleasant to be relieved of the burden of deciding things, and even death, insofar as it cannot be controlled, offers a certain security. But knowledge once stolen cannot be returned, as Adam and Eve discovered.

II

Now let us turn directly to the concept of political power.* Since we are interested in choice, decision, and purposeful action, we are not concerned with the sort of power an engine is said to have, or with the force exerted by a lever. In the most general sense, the sort of power we wish to analyze is the ability to make and enforce decisions. *Political* power, then, can best be understood as the power to make and enforce decisions with regard to matters of major social importance. (Hence the necessity of introducing this admittedly vague term.) It is tempting, but I think mistaken, to define political power in terms of access to, or control of, the formal institutions of law and government in a society. The trouble with such a definition is that it manages to beg the very questions about the real locus of political power

* The analysis developed in this section is quite similar in some respects to Robert Dahl's analysis of the concept of power in his essay, "The Concept of Power," *Behavioral Science,* July, 1957. Although I have very great differences with Professor Dahl on the nature of political power, particularly as it manifests itself in contemporary America, I would be remiss in failing to acknowledge the precision and subtlety of his essay. In later sections of this chapter I shall try to indicate just where we part company.

which our analysis is designed to answer. We must not assume in advance that those who control the legal and governmental institutions of a modern state exercise effective power of decision over virtually all the matters of major social importance which are objects of decision at all. That may be true, but we wish to define political power in such a way that it becomes an empirical truth and not a trivial tautology. It is at least logically possible that the locus of such power be elsewhere than in the halls of government, for example in the meeting rooms of corporate directorates if some radical critics of American society are right. By defining political power as the ability to make and enforce decisions concerning matters of major social importance, we leave it open whether political power has anything at all to do with what is ordinarily called politics.

When I introduced the notion of a matter of major social importance, I pointed out that it was both vague and relative to the interests and values of the society. In addition to this, it is also unavoidably *evaluative*. Since most contemporary social scientists aspire to the condition of methodological grace known as value-neutrality, it might be worth devoting a few words to defending a definition of political power which rests on a frankly non-value-neutral concept.

The dispute over the thesis of the power elite obviously involves some sorts of assumptions about the relative importance of various matters of decision. No one in his right mind would attempt to refute the claim that Stalin was a dictator by pointing out that millions of Russian citizens made countless individual decisions about when to rise, whom to marry, and what to eat. The point is that so far as politics is concerned, Stalin made more decisions about *important* matters than anyone else did, and he showed himself capable of enforcing his decisions against opposition from other

major political figures in Russian society. But suppose
someone argued that Congress, in the past decade, had made
virtually no decisions about matters of truly major importance, and that instead the power of decision had shifted
completely to the President and his Administration. Those
who rank the Cuban missile crisis, the Cuban invasion, and
the Vietnam war far above the assortment of New Frontier
and Great Society social legislation in importance might
agree with this judgment, and they might conclude that the
relative inability of Congress to call the turn in military and
foreign policy meant an end to genuine parliamentary democracy in America. Those, on the other hand, who assigned
greater importance to the domestic developments of recent
years might insist that Congress retained significant power
over matters of major social importance, and hence possessed considerable political power. To some extent, of
course, the dispute is over facts: Does the mood of Congress restrain the President more severely in foreign policy
than appears on the surface? Will the social legislation have
no lasting effect on American life, or is it the first wave of a
tide which will transform America? But at bottom, there
is an ineradicable evaluative dimension to the argument.
Radicals and liberals are not so far apart in their values as,
say, Bolsheviks and Czarists, but they do genuinely disagree.
Hence any dispute between them about the nature and location of political power will in part be a dispute over what
is important, what is worth trying to control, in modern
society.

Faced with this necessity of introducing value judgments into the very foundations of his work, the liberal
social scientist is liable to attempt to retreat into "objectivity." The consequence, unfortunately, is merely that he re-
places his own evaluations with what Galbraith so acutely
labels the "conventional wisdom." He simply adopts unthink-

ingly the *consensus gentium* of the moment. If everyone is talking about the decisions of war and peace, he studies the process of decision in the Pentagon. When interest shifts to urban renewal, he launches a foundation-supported investigation of the dynamics of City Hall politics. One of the curious effects of this false objectivity is the creation of the myth that the liberal center is populated by objective, value-neutral seekers after the truth, whereas the right and left wings are manned by impassioned (and hence biased) crusaders whose study of society is motivated by a quite unscientific moral concern. The truth, as Max Weber pointed out some time ago, is that every investigation of social phenomena involves some evaluative judgment as to which problems, distinctions, categories are important. The very concept of a "power elite" presupposes, as we shall see, some assumptions about how power should be distributed in a society. A political scientist could as easily discuss political power in America without making some judgments about what is and is not important as an art historian could discuss the history of art without making some judgments about what is and is not beautiful.

III

We are finally in a position to examine the dispute over the thesis of the power elite. Drawing on the definitions and clarifications that we have just developed, we can define a power elite as *a group of persons who together decide most of the matters of major social importance which are objects of anyone's decision at all*. If, in addition, this group exhibits the familiar marks of social cohesion, including common origins, interlocking familial alliances, common life-styles, educational experiences, and economic level, we may call them a Ruling Class. Such a class need not be hereditary, although experience suggests that it will do its best to make itself so. But at the very least, entry to its ranks must be by cooptation rather than independent effort, so that it can truly be said to control its membership and its perpetuation. Nor need this elite be fully self-conscious of itself as such; group- or class-consciousness is hardly a necessary condition for the existence of a ruling class. And it goes without saying that the members of the elite need not be partners to anything resembling a *conspiracy*. The concept of a power elite, or ruling class, is an objective concept purporting to describe the actual distribution of political power, not a subjective concept characterizing men's beliefs about that distribution.

Very simply, then, C. Wright Mills maintains that the United States is ruled by a power elite which exhibits many, if not all, of the characteristics of a ruling class. Most of the decisions concerning matters of major social importance are made by this elite, which operates sometimes in full view, sometimes behind the scenes. The decision-making activities of supposed power centers such as Congress are limited to matters of middling social importance. There are a great many such decisions, to be sure, but neither individually nor in sum do they amount to much. The real power—which is to say, the power of decision over matters of *major* importance—is vested in a relatively small group of men occupying the "command posts" of industry, the military establishment, and the Administration.* The ruling elite is not a cabal or a clique; it may even be torn by internal dissension. *Nevertheless*, it has a common political

---

* Notice that one cannot even formulate the power elite thesis without committing oneself to evaluation of the relative social importance of various objects of decision. No one denies that *some* decisions lie outside the control of Congress; the question is only whether all the *important* decisions do. Note also, contrary to the beliefs of many "objectivist" liberals, that it is impossible to *deny* the thesis unless one makes some contrary evaluative commitments.

ideology, pursues a single broad line of policy, exhibits considerable social cohesion, and circulates its membership more and more freely among the top positions of the several hierarchies of power. Generals move into presidential politics and corporate directorates, industrial magnates take key cabinet posts, top politicians become corporate directors. Entrance into the elite is partially hereditary, partially by cooptation. Despite the appearance of democratic forms in the distribution and exercise of power, American politics is in fact the sovereign domain of this self-perpetuating elite. It is only marginally responsible at best to the people it purports to serve, and it employs a variety of coercive and persuasive devices to protect itself from invasion from below.

Mills' book provoked considerable response, to put it mildly.[*] Despite some praise from other radical critics of the American dream, the reviews were predominantly negative. Liberals advanced three sorts of objections to Mills' thesis: first, it was argued that he left the concept of power unanalyzed and unprovided with operational tests for its application; second, Mills' account of the concentration of political power in the hands of a small elite was rejected as empirically false—quite to the contrary, *power* could be seen to be divided into countervailing *powers* or distributed among competing interest groups; and finally, by concentrating on the social origins and status insignia of his "elite" instead of examining the process of decision-making in which they engaged, Mills allowed himself to ignore the degree to which the major decisions reflected either a common social interest or else a confluence of competing group

[*] Recently, G. William Domhoff and Hoyt B. Ballard have collected a number of critical reviews of *The Power Elite*, together with Mills' reply, and some comments by themselves, in *C. Wright Mills and the Power Elite* (Boston: Beacon Press, 1968). Following Mills, they group the critics as liberals, radicals, and highbrows.

and private interests. It was also pointed out by a number of critics that Mills drew his examples of decisions by the power elite exclusively from the area of foreign and military affairs, where decisions are vested constitutionally not even in an elite or ruling class but in one man, the President, and his advisers.

Since the initial dispute, something of a radical counter-reply has been developed by social critics who admired Mills' work but felt that it needed buttressing. Ignoring the first objection, they have presented two sorts of arguments in support of Mills. The claims concerning the concentration of political power have been defended by studies both of local communities, particularly in the big urban centers where Negro populations are denied access to the centers of power and decision, and also of such high policy decisions as the dropping of the atom bomb on Japan, the rearmament of the United States in the fifties, and the progressive escalation of the war in Vietnam. The pluralist model of competing and countervailing interest groups has been denied any relevance to either the highest or the lowest levels of decision-making. And in the past decade, it has been at those two levels, rather than at the intermediate level of Congressional decision, that the most pressing social problems have arisen.

At the same time, a number of authors have come forward with detailed statistical justifications of Mills' rather impressionistic portrait of the "higher circles." Studies of the distribution of wealth, career lines, educational and social habits, and residential patterns in American society are offered to confirm Mills' claim that the occupants of the seats of power constitute something approaching a genuine social class.

Without engaging in a full-scale review of the literature, let me simply offer my judgment that here, as in many

other cases, the factual disputes remain inconclusive because of a prior failure to clarify the central concepts of the
disagreement.* In Chapter 4, I shall offer my estimate of
the strengths and weaknesses of the pluralist theory of
American democracy. In the present chapter, therefore, I
shall concentrate the remainder of my discussion on the conceptual unclarities of the notion of a power elite. Anticipat-
ing somewhat, I shall try to show that the liberals are right
to deny the existence of a power elite, but they are right
for the wrong reasons. Mills and the radicals, by contrast, are
wrong, but in a sense they are wrong for the right reasons.
I trust that this conclusion will not seem too much like a
cautious stroll down the middle of the road.

The best attack on the concept of the power elite from
the liberal camp was mounted by Robert Dahl. In an essay
entitled "A Critique of the Ruling Elite Model," appearing
a year after the analysis of "The Concept of Power" cited
above, Dahl suggests some ways in which the notion of a
ruling elite could be transformed into an operational concept with explicit criteria of confirmation and disconfirma-
tion. Although Dahl merely formulates possible criteria
and concludes the essay with the modest remark that the
evidence for an American power elite has not yet been
examined, he quite clearly doubts that Mills or anyone else
can find adequate empirical confirmation for the dramatic
claims advanced by the radical critics.

In order to make sense of the hypothesis that some men
have power over others, Dahl argues, it is necessary first to
specify the scope of the power (i.e., the set of objects of decision, in my terminology). Dahl employs, unanalyzed, the
notion of "key political issues" as a way of delineating the
scope of the power elite theory. If I understand him cor-

---

* A similar confusion vitiated the debates over political loyalty, as we
saw in the previous chapter.

rectly, Dahl means by a "key political issue" something rather like what I mean by a "matter of major social importance," except that his language obscures the fact previously mentioned that a matter of major social importance may not be decided in the *political* arena. This point is not important in Dahl's theoretical analysis, since one can easily enough substitute "matter of major social importance" for "key political decision." In his empirical work, however, Dahl seems to me to make precisely the illegitimate assumption I sought to avoid. Both in *Who Governs?* and in "The Concept of Power," he simply takes it for granted that the important decisions are all made within the *political* sphere; what is even more questionable, he assumes without argument that the key political issues are to be found among those matters which have actually been decided by someone. This permits Dahl to rule out in advance, without consideration, all questions about why certain matters of major social importance failed to become objects of decision at all.

Within the sphere of key political decisions, Dahl argues that the concept of power can be given operational meaning only if there are disagreements over the issues. To say that a group has power with regard to an issue is to say that its preference prevails over the conflicting preferences of others. If there is some group of individuals whose preferences "regularly prevail in . . . all cases of disagreement over key political issues," then we may speak of that group as a *controlling group* (though not quite as a power elite, as we shall see). The point is that if no differences in preference are ever manifested in the society over matters of major social importance, or alternatively if the only "conflict" is between preference on the one hand and indifference on the other, then there is no empirical method for getting evidence of the exercise of power. In effect, Dahl is arguing that our earlier definition of a "power elite" is wrong. A power elite is *not* merely a group of persons who together decide the matters of major importance which are objects of anyone's decision at all. Such a group might properly be called a decisory group, but not a power elite. In order to qualify as a power elite, a group must regularly *prevail* in the making and enforcing of such decisions as are taken with regard to matters of major social importance. And if our concepts are to be truly operational, we must present evidence of the existence of opposition to the prevailing group. It is not enough to *assume* that those who decide in ways we dislike must have done so in the face of significant opposition.

Dahl now advances one further qualification before offering his definition of a power elite. Since this qualification, in a suitably revised and expanded form, will play a central role in my argument, I shall quote Dahl's statement at length:

> In a full-fledged democracy acting strictly according to majority rule, the majority would constitute a controlling group, even though the individual members of the majority might change from one issue to the next. But since our model is to represent a ruling elite system, we require that these be *less than a majority*. However, in any representative system with single member voting districts where more than two candidates receive votes, a candidate *could* win with less than a majority of the votes; and it is possible, therefore, to imagine a truly sovereign legislature elected under the strictest "democratic" rules that was nonetheless governed by a legislative majority representing the first preferences of a minority of voters. Yet I do not think we would want to call such a system a ruling elite system. Because of this kind of difficulty, I propose that we exclude from our definition of a ruling elite any controlling group that is a product of rules that are

actually followed (that is, "real" rules) under which a
majority of individuals could dominate if they took certain actions permissible under the "real" rules. In short,
to constitute a ruling elite a controlling group must not
be *a pure artifact of democratic rules.**

I suspect that many radical proponents of the power
elite thesis would react with impatience to this sort of qualification. Of course we aren't talking about some duly elected
government! they would protest. Anyone who has lived in
the United States in recent years knows perfectly well that
there are some who rule and others who are ruled. These
definitional maneuvers and refutations of straw-man theses
cannot change the plain facts! So they might argue—but they
would be wrong. Dahl's clarifications are both legitimate and
relevant; indeed, they need to be generalized and extended
before the power elite thesis can be definitively evaluated.

There are a number of types of minority rule which
clearly are *not* what social critics have in mind when they
complain of the existence of a power elite. Dahl cites the
case of rule by a democratically elected government which,
under the rules of the system, represents a minority of
the voters. The point, of course, is that in such a system, the
majority could perfectly well rule if it chose to do so. The
minority "rules" because there is sufficient division among
the electorate to deny any party an absolute majority of
votes. Consider now a somewhat different sort of case. Suppose that in a free, democratically organized society there
was a man (or a group of men) whose grasp of the issues and
political wisdom was widely believed to be superior to that
of the general run of citizens. Suppose, indeed, that this
man, by the force of his arguments and the elevation of his
vision, regularly persuaded the electorate to support his
preference. Imagine that he was returned to the office of

* Dahl, op. cit., pp. 27–28 in Domhoff and Ballard.

president term after term, and that he and his colleagues had virtually a free hand in the making and execution of public policy. Now, this situation might be very frustrating indeed to the small band who opposed his policies, believing his vision to be distorted and his arguments meretricious. In exasperation at their inability to dissuade their countrymen from following such a leader, they might grow extravagant in their condemnations, until they denounced him as dictator, and tyrant. They might feel bound in conscience to defy the government even to the extent of violent attempts at its overthrow. But surely it would be very odd indeed for them to accuse the ruler and his colleagues of being a power elite. If the authority of the rulers rests on the persuasiveness (not necessarily the truth) of their arguments, they can hardly be said to have coerced their followers! One might as well accuse Einstein of tyranny for having so thoroughly converted physicists and mathematicians to the general theory of relativity.

Consider yet another case (which Dahl also briefly discusses). Suppose that a ruling group regularly wins power in free democratic elections with the support of very much less than a majority of the eligible voters, merely because most of the electorate is indifferent to the entire political process and fails to exercise its franchise. We may even suppose that there is considerable competition *among* elites for control of the government, but only within the framework of a broad consensus on fundamental questions of policy. Here again the unsuccessful opposition, on the fringes of the political system, may decry the lack of real debate and the stultifying continuity of wrongheaded policies from administration to administration. But so long as they have every opportunity to proselytize for votes among the great mass of the uncommitted, they can hardly blame their failure on a "power elite."

Let us distinguish two general sorts of opposition which a government may face. *Constitutional* opposition is any sort of opposition to the policies or to the tenure of the rulers which is permitted by the "real rules" of the system, as Dahl calls them. In the American political system, the fundamental power of constitutional opposition is the right periodically to vote the government out of office. The various powers of Congress to check the Administration and of the courts to check both come under the heading of constitutional opposition. So do such informal and undefined powers as the State Department's ability to transform the President's explicit directives for change into authorizations of operational immobility, or the ability of legislative assistants to shape the policy predilections of the Congressmen they serve. *Violent* opposition, by contrast, is opposition which breaks the real rules of the system. Insurrections, revolutions, military coups, assassinations are obvious examples of violent opposition to a ruling group.

The distinction's value lies in reminding us that a government may be invulnerable to one sort of opposition and yet exceedingly vulnerable to another. The President of the United States is probably as secure as any ruler in history against the threat of revolution or coup. Yet he is only moderately secure against assassination, and on noon of the Inauguration Day of his successor there is virtually nothing he can do to protect himself against a sudden and total loss of political power. By contrast, there are Latin American dictators who are invulnerable to constitutional challenge but in constant mortal danger of violent overthrow.

IV

Let us attempt a new definition of the concept of a power elite, in the light of the qualifications and limitations that have just been advanced. A power elite, I suggest, should be understood as *a group of persons who together decide most of the matters of major social importance which are objects of anyone's decision at all, and who are capable of enforcing their decision against widespread opposition of either a violent or a constitutional nature.* A well-entrenched dictator together with his administrative and military entourage is a power elite (but not the dictator alone, unless he is able to win out against an organized palace revolt). A duly elected President together with his Administration is *not* a power elite so long as it is possible to remove him from office by such ordinary means as not reelecting him.

This is a loaded definition, needless to say. By including the qualification that the ruling group must be able to enforce its decisions against widespread constitutional opposition, I appear to have begged the question whether America is controlled by a power elite, for not even C. Wright Mills denies that an organized majority of ordinary citizens could change the direction of our foreign and domestic policy virtually overnight, if it chose to act. With the exception of one possible argument, which will be considered shortly, there appears to be no ground for claiming that America is ruled by the sort of power elite which I have just defined. Why then should we adopt this definition?

In Talmudic fashion, let me answer a question with a question. Why did Mills write *The Power Elite*? Why have critics of American society seized upon the phrase, and why have those liberal political scientists whom Mills justly accused of a "celebration" of American politics so hotly rejected it? Mills did not intend the term as a morally neutral category of descriptive political science. One might as easily imagine an anthropologist classifying the marital customs of primitive tribes as "monogamous, adulterous, and promiscuous." The phrase "power elite" was an accusation flung at a smug and self-righteous America which prided itself,

wrongly Mills believed, on having successfully embodied
the ideals and principles of democracy in its ongoing political institutions. In the opening pages of his book, Mills defines the power elite as "those who are able to realize their
will, *even if others resist it*" (page 9, emphasis added). Presumably he means, even if a large part, indeed a majority,
of the population resist. If Mills is talking about anything
at all, he is talking about a society in which a small group
are able to enforce their will against the opposition of some
considerable portion of the rest. Mills has moral objections
to such a society simply because it places power in the hands
of the few rather than in the hands of the many. He blames
the few, presumably, because they use force, wealth, propaganda, or trickery to preserve that power in the face of legitimate opposition from a majority of the citizens. Liberals
reject the epithet "power elite" because in general they ap-
prove of the way in which power is distributed and exercised
in the United States.

Now we can, if we choose, define "power elite" to mean
simply "a group of men who make all or most of the major
decisions in a society," omitting the qualification concerning
the sorts of opposition they are able to overcome. But if we
do so, we shall be guilty of promoting what Charles Steven-
son has called a "persuasive definition." That is, we shall be
using a term which has acquired a certain moral flavor of
condemnation, while redefining it to eliminate *precisely* the
component which originally gave it that flavor. After all, if
the ruling group in a society maintains its position by free
elections, or by persuasion, or through the indifference of
the remainder of the population, why *should* we condemn
it for making the decisions about matters of major social
importance? To be sure, we may condemn the *decisions* they
make, as we may condemn those of a popular government
or even those of the people as a whole. But a ruling group

does not become a "power elite," with all that implies about the usurpation of power and the illegitimate exercise of authority, merely by making wrong—even wicked—decisions. Only a romantic with an abiding faith in the goodness of The People will assume that when a society makes bad decisions, the fault *must* lie with an illegitimate and antidemocratic elite.

What is the present distribution of power in America? This is not the place to launch a full-scale investigation of such a question, and I certainly have no intention of bringing my discussion to a standstill while I laboriously canvass the vast literature that has grown up on the subject. Nevertheless, I think a few obvious things can be said which may permit us to arrive at a provisional conclusion on the power elite debate.

In the United States today, a relatively small group of men make virtually all the decisions concerning those matters of major social importance which are objects of decision at all. Most of them—the President and major Administration figures, the key Senators and Congressmen, the few influential Governors or Mayors, the senior military officials—are public employees whose power is directly derived from their official position. Some—the top echelons of the corporate world and their counterparts in the great foundations—derive such power as they have from their relatively brief tenure in the presidencies and chairmanships of their organizations. Only a very few are powerful in virtue of their personal wealth, and even they transform their money into power principally by buying the means for influencing elections.

But this group of powerful men, although it originates most of the major political decisions in American society, is remarkably vulnerable to large-scale popular opposition from the ranks of the "ordinary man," as Mills calls the rest of us. All the public officials among them, including those military men who rise to positions of political power, are either elected by the people or else are appointed by those who are elected. Hence a massive shift, right or left, in the distribution of voters along the political spectrum would be reflected almost immediately in a radical redirection of decision-making. The image we are encouraged by Mills to entertain is that of a conspiratorial clique foisting its policies on a society which either actively opposes them or else is kept in such a state of ignorance and disorganization that its disapproval can never develop into effective opposition. But the facts are quite different, as even the most casual observer of the American scene can see. Radical candidates, for example, have run in countless elections around the United States. They receive a measure of publicity and exposure which is surely in excess of their proportionate share of the votes, although of course much below what is accorded the major party candidates. The elections are free and secret—not even the most disenchanted radical critics claim otherwise. The result is that they rarely win more than two percent of the total vote! In Massachusetts, candidates have been known to do better than that merely by taking the name of Kennedy! It is natural to be discouraged, even bitter, in the face of such popular reaction. I have found that a stint in the Peace Movement is more likely to turn a man to Swift than to Marx. But it is surely wrong to explain the unresponsiveness of the American voter by invoking a power elite. The fact, of course, is that since this supposed elite is headed by men whose primary desire is to be elected, a large enough bloc of voters could turn them in almost any political direction.

The only segment of the group of powerful men whose power base is independent of the voters is the corporate directors. Their power derives from their control of the major corporations, which are not in turn responsible to the people. Now, some of the power of big business in the United States comes from its ability to affect the decisions of Congress and the Administration, through campaign contributions, influence in regulatory agencies, and so forth. But the important question for our purposes is whether business also exercises power *outside* the normal channels of government. Clearly, the great corporations regularly make decisions whose consequences are of the utmost social importance. These decisions, furthermore, are not subject to review by the general public, as are the decisions of elected or appointed officials. *But although the unregulated decisions of big business have consequences of major social importance, those consequences themselves are rarely objects of decision.* The reason for this is simply that capital in the United States is so fragmented into administratively autonomous corporations that such matters of major social importance as total yearly investment in heavy industry, new housing starts, economy-wide inventory levels, and so on, are not objects of anyone's decision at all. Some relatively unimportant efforts at collusion are undertaken by executives, particularly within single industries. But nothing like economic planning takes place in the United States, and hence no one can be said to exercise power over the corporate economy. (Private power, that is. The federal government makes a number of decisions about taxation, etc., which have some effect on the economy as a whole, but of course those decisions are subject to monitoring by the electorate.)

There is considerable difference between a *power elite* and an *establishment*. Both are groups of men who monopolize the making of decisions about matters of major social importance, but a power elite is capable of enforcing its decisions against considerable opposition of either a violent or a constitutional nature, whereas an establishment rules, as it were, by a mixture of propaganda, persuasion, and apathy. The United States is ruled by an establishment which is, in the terms of William Kornhauser, "highly accessible."* That is, the rulers are quite responsive to pressures from the ruled, and entrance into the elite is relatively open, although of course restricted in numbers. The truly powerful men in America are not, save by accident, the sons of powerful men, nor are they drawn from any single region or social class. Through their control over the procedures by which young men rise in the political, military, or corporate hierarchies, the men at the top exercise a considerable control over the character and policies of their successors. Nevertheless, they are virtually powerless to obstruct for long a policy which commands widespread, *active,* popular support.

To see that this is so, let us try to imagine what would happen in America today if there were suddenly to develop an enormous groundswell of vigorous support for a domestic policy of full-scale socialism and planned economy. We may suppose this policy to be violently opposed by virtually the entire establishment of politicians, generals, corporate executives, foundation presidents, university heads, and so forth, and yet supported by the people. The first evidence of the change in public opinion might be a weird set of answers to the usual Gallup or Harris polls. Initially, social scientists would issue complex explanations stressing the limitations of sampling as a technique of research, the finite probability of a skewed result, and so forth. Then a minor socialist candidate might win a state election. Immediately, the prospective candidates would appear, encouraged by this straw in the wind. As socialist victories piled up, politicians would begin to reconsider their positions, and businessmen would hedge their bets by making small, private contributions to socialist campaign funds. By the next national election, a

* William Kornhauser, *The Politics of Mass Society.*

sizable group of socialist representatives would sit in Congress. It could hardly take more than half a dozen years before a full socialist ticket swept to power and captured the presidency.

Is there anyone who really believes that "the establishment" would try to block this political transformation by such illegal means as voiding elections, refusing to relinquish office, calling out the troops to brutalize and intimidate voters? We shall probably never have a chance to find out, alas, but it seems evident to me that in the face of an aroused citizenry bent upon instituting even so un-American a policy as socialism, the established rulers of American society would be quite powerless. The fact is that Americans are ruled by default. No people in history has ever manacled itself so willingly, so knowledgeably, so docilely, in the chains of tyranny.

The principal complaint of radical critics is not that the American political system is unresponsive to the wishes of the people, but that the policies of its rulers are wrong. That may indeed be true—I think it is—but it is hardly by itself evidence of the existence of a power elite.

I remarked earlier that there was one possible argument in support of the thesis that America is controlled by a power elite. It is often claimed that the apparent power of the electorate has been nullified by the control of information and propaganda exercised by the elite. The voters have it within their power to determine the major political decisions, but, it is said, they are systematically misled, lied to, and indoctrinated through the mass media and in the schools. Public support is artificially generated for policies whose true purposes are never revealed. Those who rebel against this manipulated consensus either are coopted into the system with lucrative and prestigious jobs, or else are denied a hearing so that their protest is robbed of any real political significance.

Despite the popularity of this explanation of the passivity and acquiescence of the American electorate, it is in my opinion totally unsupported by the facts. Indeed, it is so manifestly implausible that its popularity with radicals requires an explanation, which I will try presently to provide. As proof of the falsity of the indoctrination theory, let us consider the issue which has dominated American politics for the past several years—Vietnam.

The official government justification of our Vietnamese policy has been regularly and explicitly refuted by news reports for almost two years now. The dictatorial character of the South Vietnamese military junta is displayed nightly in televised news broadcasts which reach tens of millions of American homes. Vivid images of the torturing of captives, the suppression of Buddhist groups, the burning of villages, are forced upon the American consciousness. News commentators repeatedly remind their audiences of the chasm between the predictions of our military advisers and the actual course of events. The hostile questioning of Administration witnesses by dissenting senators preempts revenue-producing afternoon and evening programs, so that Americans are virtually forced to acquaint themselves with the anti-government views of highly respected political figures. Those citizens whose political interest prompts them to even the slightest effort need only pick up the *New York Times* to read condemnations of the war as vigorous as any published in left-wing journals of protest. The bookstands are crowded with more dissenting literature on the subject than anyone could want to read.

How was the Johnson Administration able to persist for so long in its policies in the face of this dissenting propaganda? The answer is painfully clear: the anti-war forces simply did not have the votes! So long as the United States was not obviously losing the war, and the costs were marginal to the economy and inflicted principally on the poor and politically silent segment of the population, the great mass of the American people were too stupid, or too vicious, to be very much concerned by the fact that their government was systematically murdering the inhabitants of Vietnam in order to support a petty dictatorship and maintain a military presence in Southeast Asia. As the costs of the war increased and the battle turned against us, the American people slowly moved from enthusiastic support to passive acquiescence to tentative opposition. In response to this shift, Johnson finally altered his policy and made the peace moves which had so long been urged. But the evidence of the Dominican Republic and elsewhere does very strongly suggest that if the murder could have been continued at a sufficiently low cost, no significant segment of the American population could ever have been mobilized against it. Even the Germans, we may suppose, would have turned against the extermination of the Jews if they had realized how much precious war materiel was being diverted from the battle front to carry out that policy.*

---

* It is worth pointing out that Kennedy and Johnson were originally prompted to become involved in Vietnam precisely because they believed that such operations could be carried out inexpensively and effectively. Early in the Kennedy administration, Secretary McNamara rejected the Air Force first-strike nuclear policy and adopted instead the Army-Navy second-strike policy of creating a nuclear deterrence umbrella beneath which the struggle for the so-called Third World could go on. The theory was that within the context of a nuclear stalemate, limited wars and paramilitary operations would carry little or no danger of a nuclear war. McNamara recognized that such limited operations would be political as well as military, and so he created the system of "counterinsurgency" forces which were to act as highly mobile, specialized, politically sophisticated units in revolutionary situations around the world. New weapons were invented to accompany the new tactics, including the helicopters so much in evidence in Vietnam. The premise of the theory proved correct—

If the United States is not in the grip of a power elite, why do so many radical critics lean to that theory? There are a number of reasons, including the natural inclination to relieve one's frustrations by pinning the blame for failure on some identifiable villain. But the fundamental explanation, I think, is that the radical impulse feeds on a faith in the natural goodness of the people. If the state is permitted to act wickedly, it must be because the people are in chains. If there are no visible chains, then there must be invisible chains of ignorance or a habit of servitude. If the people are not tyrannized, it must be that they have been brainwashed. Otherwise they would exercise their power and dethrone the rulers. Now up to a point, there is a rationale for this faith. Insofar as the wicked policies of the rulers thwart the interests of the people (even, if you will, the *true* interests of the people), we may assume that natural human self-interest would lead the people to oppose those policies. If there is no overt opposition, we may reasonably infer that the people are denied the chance, or else that they as yet lack a true understanding of the nature of their rulers. We may even be forced to conclude, as Rousseau did two centuries ago, that slavery long enough imposed can become a habit, and that real liberation requires more than the physical striking off of chains.

---

the nuclear stalemate, strengthened by the Soviet Union's remarkably pacific foreign policy, has allowed a variety of limited military operations to be conducted with no real threat of nuclear war. But the heart of the theory has turned out to be quite wrong, as anyone with the slightest understanding of the revolutions of the Third World could have predicted. The "insurgents" simply cannot be put down quickly and quietly by small, well-equipped special units. Those among us who still value freedom and justice can give thanks that McNamara's calculations were mistaken. If it had proved feasible to stifle revolutions cheaply, we can be quite sure that the United States would have put down every threat of social change as quickly as it overturned the Dominican government, and with as little outcry from the American people.

But if the policies of the ruling elite *do not* seriously frustrate the interests of a majority of the people—if those policies are merely immoral, as is our foreign policy, or oppressive only to a minority, as is our treatment of the poor and ghetto dwellers in this country—then there is no very good reason to expect even an educated public to reject them. Half a century ago, European socialists discovered that national loyalties bound the working classes of England, Germany, and France more strongly than the fragile ties of class unity. Today, rational argument and overwhelming evidence seem to make very little impact on the American people, even when they are exposed to both in the most forceful manner possible.

To all this, the radical will reply that the analysis remains at too superficial a level. There is no direct manipulation of the masses through centrally controlled newspapers and television networks. The United States is not, like Red China, a nation in which daily life is conducted to the accompaniment of blaring loudspeakers and ritual readings of the words of the great leader. The control is more subtle. It operates through the images and language in which school children are taught about the American past or current affairs. People's minds are molded by the endless repetition of such ideologically biased phrases as "the free world," "the Communist menace," and "the iron curtain." Just as no one has to be told that the cowboys in a western are the good guys and the Indians are the bad guys, so no explicit indoctrination is needed to convey the established world-view of the cold war as a struggle between American goodness and Communist evil. The ruling elite in America endures, despite the facade of democratic institutions, because it shapes the way in which Americans perceive the world, thereby predetermining their apparently unfettered responses to the political choices put before them.

There may indeed be some truth in this argument, although the minds of Americans must be very feeble indeed if they can be manipulated and perverted by such mild and ineffectual propaganda as is served up in public schools and newspapers. But, at best, the argument only explains the orientation of American political thought. It explains, that is to say, why Americans should as a group lie so far to the right of Englishmen or Swedes in the political spectrum. What it does *not* show is that this fact can be traced to the deliberate choice of any identifiable group of rulers. The tone and bias of the public discourse in America is a consequence of countless deliberate decisions, no one of which comes close to determining the character of even a major segment of that discourse. The tone is one of those matters of major social importance which are not themselves objects of anyone's decision. To see that this is so, one need simply contrast the American experience with that of a genuine totalitarian dictatorship in which the content of the mass media can be clearly traced to the explicit decisions of specifiable individuals.

What shall we say about the dispute between the radicals and the liberals? The radicals say that America is ruled by a power elite, and they are wrong. Those who rule in this country do so by default. They are completely vulnerable to popular opposition of even the most peaceful sort. But radicals are right to be outraged by the quality of America's political life and by the direction of her domestic and foreign policies. They are frustrated by their failure to persuade the American people of even the simplest moral truths—that it is wrong to burn peasant huts in Asia on the pretext of protecting free elections in San Francisco; that the rights of investment capital do not take precedence over the rights of men; that the oppressed inhabitants of urban ghettoes have as much right to burn the stores in which they have been

cheated as the revolutionary Bostonians had to jettison tea
on which they would not pay an unjust tax. And in their
frustration, radicals succumb to the temptation to blame the
rulers rather than those who passively permit themselves to
be ruled.

The liberals deny that America is ruled by a power elite,
and they are right. But having won their little victory over
the radicals, they then rejoice in the moral disaster of American politics, calling it stability, and moderation, and the end
of ideology. They congratulate one another on the lack of
moral passion in our political life, much like maiden school
mistresses confusing a deficiency of libido with good man-
ners. Their powers of social imagination are exhausted by
the thought of extending to Negroes those inequalities and
disadvantages already suffered by white Americans. But it
makes no more sense to blame the chroniclers of our political apathy than the beneficiaries of it. The fault lies neither
with liberal political scientists nor with the established order
of decision makers, but simply with the American people.

v

America is not ruled by a power elite. But that is hardly the
end of the matter. The most significant fact about the distribution of power in America is not who makes such decisions as are made, but rather how many matters of the
greatest social importance are not objects of anyone's decision at all. It is universally agreed, for example, that the
welfare of the nation depends upon a stable rate of economic growth, and yet virtually everyone is content to restrict the government to the most feeble sorts of indirect
economic controls. Americans seem willing to allow their
cities to decay into unintended slums despite the existence
of more than enough theoretical understanding of the problem to permit rational and deliberate solutions to be initi-

ated. There is no significant body of socialist thought in America today, which is to say that American intellectuals accept a condition of social irrationality which is unnecessary and therefore inexcusable. The responsibility for this lamentable state of affairs belongs at least in part to those liberal social philosophers who have written so contemptuously and dismissively of the utopian style in social criticism.

There are two kinds of social criticism, corresponding to the two kinds of rationality discussed earlier. The first, much celebrated by liberals as eminently "practical" and very much in the spirit of anti-theoretical American pragmatism, consists of proposals for improving on the manner in which decisions are made concerning matters which are already objects of decision. Such criticism has the virtue of "relevance." That is to say, it speaks directly to someone who is already making decisions and tells him, Do this rather than that. At best, it is capable of raising a society to the highest peak on that plateau of rationality which the society has already reached. But it is not capable of carrying the society forward to a genuinely new level of rationality. Hence it produces great success in the treatment of some social problems, and none at all in the treatment of others.

We might compare such criticism to the medical prescriptions offered by the very best doctors before the discovery of the bacterial origins of disease. There was a good deal that could be done by those doctors through diet, rest, and natural remedies, and whatever their limitations it was obviously better to be in their hands than those of a quack. But some diseases simply do not respond to bed rest and diet. The doctors who recognized their bacterial causes and found antibiotics to treat them moved the whole discipline of medicine to a new level. Diseases became treatable which were simply beyond control before; in other words, they became for the first time objects of medical decision.

In social theory, the criticism which produces this sort of qualitative advance is called "utopian." It consists in searching for ways to transform into new objects of social decision those matters of importance which are not within anyone's power at present. Each such discovery is a major advance for social rationality. In Hegel's rather dramatic phrase, it carries men out of the realm of necessity and into the realm of freedom. Naturally, proposals for transforming uncontrolled matters of importance into objects of decisions require new kinds of institutional organization, new ways of thinking, and—very possibly—new makers of decisions. Deeply entrenched habits of behavior may have to be uprooted, and inevitably some patterns of privilege are destroyed. Although it is impossible to reverse an advance in social control once it has been accomplished, there is no assurance that new advances will follow. As Robert Heilbroner points out in his recent book, *The Limits of Capitalism*, it is extremely likely that the present system of privilege and private ownership of capital will persist in the United States at least to the end of the century, which is about as far into the future as anyone can see. Despite the great and growing wealth of the American economy, the United States may see itself passed by socialist nations of East and West Europe, as it already sees itself left behind by some of them in such matters as the elimination of slums and the distribution of medical services. If it is true that some social needs, such as the reformation of our cities and the final elimination of poverty, cannot be served by even the most sophisticated maneuvers at the present level of social control, then we shall witness a progressively more frustrating failure of domestic liberalism to deal with the worsening social problems of American life. Rather like an old-time doctor who watches his pneumonia patient slip away despite his most skillful efforts, the welfare-state liberal will endlessly permute and combine the techniques which have served him in the past, only to see the slums decay and the condition of the ghetto dwellers grow more hopeless. Should this gloomy diagnosis prove correct, it may finally be borne in upon the advocates of "practical" reform that the solution lies in utopian thinking. They may see that the society requires an *increase* in power, a transforming into objects of decision of important matters which are now the consequences of un-coordinated acts, rather than merely an alteration in the way in which present power is employed.

4. Tolerance*

THE VIRTUE of a thing, Plato tells us in the *Republic,* is that state or condition which enables it to perform its proper function well. The virtue of a knife is its sharpness, the virtue of a racehorse its fleetness of foot. So too the cardinal virtues of wisdom, courage, temperance, and justice are excellences of the soul which enable a man to do well what he is meant to do, viz., to live.

As each artifact or living creature has its characteristic virtue, so we may say that each form of political society has an ideal condition, in which its guiding principle is fully realized. For Plato, the good society is an aristocracy of merit in which the wise and good rule those who are inferior in talents and accomplishment. The proper distribution of functions and authority is called by Plato "justice," and so the virtue of the Platonic utopia is justice.

* This essay first appeared under the title "Beyond Tolerance" in *A Critique of Pure Tolerance* by Robert Paul Wolff, Barrington Moore, Jr., and Herbert Marcuse (Boston: Beacon Press, 1965).

Extending this notion, we might say, for example, that the virtue of a monarchy is loyalty, for the state is gathered into the person of the king, and the society is bound together by each subject's personal duty to him. The virtue of a military dictatorship is honor; that of a bureaucratic dictatorship is efficiency. The virtue of traditional liberal democracy is equality, while the virtue of a socialist democracy is fraternity. The ideal nationalist democracy exhibits the virtue of patriotism, which is distinguished from loyalty by having the state itself as its object rather than the king.

Finally, the virtue of the modern pluralist democracy which has emerged in contemporary America is TOLERANCE. Political tolerance is that state of mind and condition of society which enables a pluralist democracy to function well and to realize the ideal of pluralism. For that reason, if we wish to understand tolerance *as a political virtue,* we must study it not through a psychological or moral investigation of prejudice, but by means of an analysis of the theory and practice of democratic pluralism.

My purpose in this chapter is to understand the philosophy of tolerance as well as to subject it to criticism. I have therefore devoted the first section entirely to an exposition of the concept as it is related to the theory of pluralism. In the second section, I explore several possible arguments for tolerance, and try to exhibit the theory of democratic pluralism as the product of a union of opposed conceptions of society and human nature. Only in the final section is the theory subjected to the criticisms which, in my opinion, make it ultimately indefensible in the contemporary age. This may at first seem a needlessly roundabout way of proceeding. I have adopted it because I see pluralism not as a thoroughly mistaken theory, but rather as a theory which played a valuable role during one stage in America's development and which has now lost its value either as description or prescription. In that sense, the present essay urges that we transcend tolerance, and as Hegel reminds us, the process of transcendence is as much an incorporation as it is a rejection.

I

Like most political theories, democratic pluralism has both descriptive and prescriptive variants. As a description, it purports to tell how modern industrial democracy—and particularly American democracy—really works. As a prescription, it sketches an ideal picture of industrial democracy as it could and should be. Both forms of the theory grew out of nineteenth-century attacks on the methodological individualism of the classical liberal tradition.

According to that tradition, political society is (or ought to be—liberalism is similarly ambiguous) an association of self-determining individuals who concert their wills and collect their power in the state for mutually self-interested ends. The state is the locus of supreme power and authority in the community. Its commands are legitimated by a democratic process of decision and control, which ensures—when it functions properly—that the subject has a hand in making the laws to which he submits. The theory focuses exclusively on the relationship between the individual citizen and the sovereign state. Associations other than the state are viewed as secondary in importance and dependent for their existence on the pleasure of the state. Some liberal philosophers counsel a minimum of state interference with private associations; others argue for active state intervention. In either case, non-governmental bodies are relegated to a subsidiary place in the theory of the state. The line of dependence is traced from the people, taken as an aggregate of unaffiliated individuals, to the state, conceived as the embodiment and representative of their collective will, to the private associations, composed of smaller groupings of those same individuals but authorized by the will of the state.

Whatever the virtues of classical liberalism as a theory of the ideal political community, it was very quickly recognized to be inadequate as a portrait of the industrial democracy which emerged in the nineteenth century. The progressively greater divergence of fact from theory could be traced to two features of the new order. The first was the effective political enfranchisement of the entire adult populations of the great nation-states; the second was the growth of an elaborate industrial system in the private sphere of society, which gave rise to a new "pluralistic" structure within the political framework of representative government.

Traditional democratic theory presupposed an immediate and evident relation between the individual citizen and the government. Whether in the form of "direct democracy," as Rousseau desired, or by means of the representative mechanism described by Locke, the state was to confront the citizen directly as both servant and master. The issues debated in the legislature would be comprehensible to every educated subject, and their relevance to his interests easily understood. With the emergence of mass politics, however, all hope of this immediacy and comprehensibility was irrevocably lost. The ideal of a small, self-governing, autonomous political society retained its appeal, finding expression in the utopian communities which sprang up in Europe and America throughout the nineteenth century. As a standard by which to judge the great industrial democracies of the new era, however, it suffered from the greatest possible failing—irrelevance. Permanent, complex institutional arrangements became necessary in order to transmit the "will of the people" to the elected governors.

At the same time, great industrial corporations appeared in the economic world and began to take the place of the old family firms. As labor unions and trade associations were organized, the classical picture of a market economy composed of many small, independent firms and a large, atomized labor supply, became less and less useful as a guide to economic reality. Individuals entered the marketplace and came in contact with one another through their associations in groups of some sort. The state in its turn brought its authority to bear on the individual only indirectly, through the medium of laws governing the behavior of those groups. It became necessary to recognize that, both politically and economically, the individual's relation to the state was mediated by a system of "middle-size" institutional associations.

The size and industrial organization alone of the modern state destroy any possibility of classical liberal democracy, for the intermediating bureaucratic organizations are necessary whether the economy is private and capitalist or public and socialist in structure. In addition, however, three factors historically more specific to the American experience have combined to produce the characteristic form which we call pluralism.

The first factor, in importance as well as in time, is the federal structure of the American system. From the birth of the nation, a hierarchy of local governments, formerly sovereign and autonomous, interposed itself between the individual and the supreme power of the state. The United States, as its name implied, was an association of political communities rather than of individuals. The natural ties of tradition and emotion binding each citizen to his native colony were reinforced by a division of powers which left many of the functions of sovereign authority to the several states. Hence the relation of the individual to the federal government was from the beginning, and even in theory, indirect and mediated by intervening bodies. Furthermore, as the eighteenth-century debates over unification reveal, the constitution took form as a series of compromises among competing interests—large states versus small, agriculture versus commerce, slaveholding versus free labor. The structure of the union was designed to balance these interests, giving each a voice but none command. The conception of politics as a conflict of more or less permanent groups was thus introduced into the foundation of our government. By implication, an individual entered the political arena principally as a member of one of those groups, rather than as an isolated agent. Conversely, the government made demands upon the individual and responded to his needs through the intercession of local authorities. As the volume of government activity grew throughout the nineteenth and twentieth centuries, this federal structure embedded itself in countless judicial and executive bodies. In America today, it is impossible to understand the organization of education, the regulation of commerce, or the precise allocation of responsibility for law enforcement without acknowledging the historically special relationship of the states to the federal government.

A second factor which has shaped the character of American democracy is our oft-chronicled penchant for dealing with social problems by means of voluntary associations. This phenomenon was made much of by Tocqueville and has since been portrayed by students of American politics as our peculiar contribution to the repertory of democratic techniques. It seems that whereas some peoples turn to God when a problem looms on the social horizon, and others turn to the state, Americans instinctively form a committee, elect a president and secretary-treasurer, and set about finding a solution on their own. The picture is idealized and more than a trifle self-congratulatory; it evokes images of the prairie or a New England town meeting, rather than a dirty industrial slum. Nevertheless, it is a fact that a remarkable variety of social needs are met in America by private and voluntary institutions, needs which in other countries would be attended to by the state. Religion, for example, is entirely a non-governmental matter because of the prohibition of an established church. The burdens of primary and secondary education are borne jointly by local governments and private institutions; higher education is dominated by the great private universities and colleges with state institutions of any sort only recently playing a significant role. The subsidy and encouragement of the arts and letters has been managed by the great charitable foundations, and until the advent of military research and development, the natural sciences found their home solely in the laboratories of universities and private industry. In addition to industry, agriculture, religion, education, art, and science, countless other dimensions of social activity have been organized on the basis of voluntary, non-governmental associations.

In order to clarify the relationship between the government and this network of private associations, we must first observe that while some groups perform their function and achieve their goal directly, others are organized as pressure groups to influence the national (or local) government and thus achieve their end indirectly. Needless to say, most associations of the first sort engage in political lobbying as well. Nevertheless, the distinction is useful, for it enables us to identify the two principal "pluralist" theories of the relationship between group and government.

The first, or "referee" theory, asserts that the role of the central government is to lay down ground rules for conflict and competition among private associations and to employ its power to make sure that no major interest in the nation abuses its influence or gains an unchecked mastery over some sector of social life. The most obvious instance is in the economic sphere, where firms compete for markets and labor competes with capital. But according to the theory a similar competition takes place among the various religions, between private and public forms of education, among different geographic regions, and even among the arts, sports, and the entertainment world for the attention and interest of the people.

The second theory might be called the "vector-sum" or "give-and-take" theory of government. Congress is seen as the focal point for the pressures which are exerted by interest groups throughout the nation, either by way of the two great parties or directly through lobbies. The laws issuing from the government are shaped by the manifold forces brought to bear upon the legislators. Ideally, Congress merely reflects these forces, combining them—or "resolving" them, as the physicists say—into a single social decision. As the strength and direction of private interests alter, there is a corresponding alteration in the composition and activity of the great interest groups—labor, big business, agriculture. Slowly, the great weathervane of government swings about to meet the shifting winds of opinion.

More important than federalism or interest-group politics in fostering the ideology of pluralism has been the impact on the American consciousness of religious, ethnic, and racial heterogeneity. Many of the original colonies were religiously orthodox communities, deliberately created in order to achieve an internal purity which was unattainable in the hostile political climate of England. The Reformation split Europe first into two, then into many, warring camps, and it was quite natural to view the nation as an association of religious communities rather than of individuals. Where some compromise could be achieved among the several sects, as eventually occurred in England, political society became in a sense a community of communities. In the United States, the deliberate prohibition of an established church made it necessary to acknowledge a diversity of religious communities within the nation. Eventually, this acceptance of heterogeneity was extended to the Roman Catholic community, and then even to the Jews.

The ethnic diversity brought about by the great immigrations of the nineteenth century produced a comparable effect in American life. The big cities especially came to be seen as agglomerations of national enclaves. Little Italys, Chinatowns, Polish ghettos, German communities, grew and flourished. America became a nation of minorities, until even the descendants of the original settlers acquired an identifying acronym, WASP.

The ethnic and religious communities in American society encountered one another through the pluralistic mechanisms of politics and private associations which already existed. The typical "hyphenated" community (Italian-American, Polish-American, etc.) had its own churches, in which the religious practices of the old country—special saints, holy days, rituals—were kept up. There were newspapers in the mother tongue, men's clubs, folk societies, businessmen's associations, trade union branches, all based on the ethnic or religious unity of the local community.

The religious and ethnic groups entered the political system at the precinct, city, or county level, using the unified mass of their voting populations as a weight to be thrown on the political scales. The decentralized, hierarchical federal structure of American government was perfectly suited to ethnic politics. The first matters of social importance which impinged on the consciousness of the group were, typically, of a sort that could be decided at the level of city government, where only a rudimentary organization and political knowledge was necessary. As Italian, Irish, Polish, or Jewish politicians ascended the ladder of elective office, they encountered the larger, multi-ethnic and multi-religious community. There they acted first as spokesmen for their own kind, and later as statesmen capable of acknowledging the greater public good.

If we draw together all these descriptive fragments, we have a portrait of pluralist democracy. America, according to this account, is a complex interlocking of ethnic, religious, racial, regional, and economic groups, whose members pursue their diverse interests through the medium of private associations, which in turn are coordinated, regulated, contained, encouraged, and guided by a federal system of representative democracy. Individual citizens confront the central government and one another as well through the intermediation of the voluntary and involuntary groups to which they belong. In this way, pluralist democracy stands in contrast to classical democracy of the liberal model; indeed, it is curiously like feudal society, in which the individual played a political role solely as a member of a guild, incorporated town, church, or estate rather than as a subject *simpliciter*. As in medieval political society, so in pluralist democracy, the guiding principle is not "one man—one vote" but rather, "every legitimate group its share." In modern America, it is taken for granted that a rough equality should be maintained between labor and business or among Catholics, Protestants, and Jews. The fact that "labor" constitutes the overwhelming majority of the population or that there are ten times as many Catholics as Jews is rarely seen as a reason for allotting influence in those proportions.

Pluralism is a theory of the way modern industrial democracies work, with particular applicability to the United States; it is also an ideal model of the way political society ought to be organized, whether in fact it is or not. As a descriptive theory, pluralism requires empirical verification, of the sort which hosts of political scientists have sought to provide in recent decades. As a normative theory, however, pluralism must be defended by appeal to some principle of virtue or ideal of the good society. In the history of the discussion of pluralism three distinct sorts of justification have been offered.

The earliest argument, dating from the preindustrial

period of religious conflict between Catholics and Protestants, Nonconformists and Anglicans, asserts that the toleration of divergent religious practices is a necessary evil, forced upon a society which either cannot suppress dissidence or else finds the social cost of suppression too high. Orthodoxy on this view is the ideal condition, intolerance of heresy even a duty in principle. It is now an historical commonplace that the great Anglo-American tradition of religious liberty can be traced to just such a grudging acceptance of *de facto* heterodoxy and not to early Protestant devotion to the freedom of individual conscience.

The second argument for pluralism presents it as a morally neutral means for pursuing political ends which cannot be achieved through traditional representative democracy. In this view, the ideal of democracy is a citizen-state, in which each man both makes the laws and submits to them. The political order is just and the people are free to the extent that each individual plays a significant and not simply symbolic role in the political process of decision. But for all the reasons catalogued above, genuine self-government is impossible in a large industrial society organized along classic democratic lines. The gulf is so broad between the rulers and the ruled that active citizen participation in the affairs of government evaporates. Even the periodic election becomes a ritual in which voters select a president whom they have not nominated to decide issues which have not even been discussed on the basis of facts which cannot be published. The result is a politics of style, of image, of faith, which is repugnant to free men and incompatible with the ideal of democracy.

But decisions will be taken, whether by democratic means or not, and so some other way than elections must be found to submit the rulers to the will of the ruled. Pluralism is offered as the answer. Within the interest groups which make up the social order, something approximating democracy takes place. These groups, in turn, through pressure upon the elected representatives, can make felt the will of their members and work out the compromises with opposed interests which would have been accomplished by debate and deliberation in a classical democracy. The government confronts not a mass of indistinguishable and ineffectual private citizens, but an articulated system of organized groups. Immediacy, effectiveness, involvement, and thus democratic participation are assured to the individual in his economic, religious, or ethnic associations—in the union local, the church, the chapter of the American Legion. Control over legislation and national policy is in turn assured to the associations through their ability to deliver votes to the legislator in an election. The politician, according to this defense of pluralism, is a middleman in the power transactions of the society. He absorbs the pressures brought to bear upon him by his organized constituents, strikes a balance among them on the basis of their relative voting strength, and then goes onto the floor of the Congress to work out legislative compromises with his colleagues, who have suffered different compositions of pressures and hence are seeking different adjustments of the competing social interests. If all goes well, every significant interest abroad in the nation will find expression, and to each will go a measure of satisfaction roughly proportional to its size and intensity. The democratic ideal of citizen-politics is preserved, for each interested party can know that through participation in voluntary, private associations, he has made his wishes felt to some small degree in the decisions of his government. To paraphrase Rousseau, the citizen is a free man since he is at least partially the author of the laws to which he submits.

The first defense of pluralism views it as a distasteful but unavoidable evil; the second portrays it as a useful means for preserving some measure of democracy under the un-promising conditions of mass industrial society. The last de-fense goes far beyond these in its enthusiasm for pluralism; it holds that a pluralistic society is natural and good and an end to be sought in itself.

The argument begins from an insight into the relation-ship between personality and society. Put simply, the idea is that the human personality, in its development, structure, and continued functioning is dependent upon the social group of which it is a significant member. The influence of society upon the individual is primarily positive, formative, supportive—indeed, indispensably so. The child who grows to manhood outside a social group becomes an animal, with-out language, knowledge, the capacity to reason, or even the ability to love and hate as other men do. As the infant is reared, he internalizes the behavior patterns and evaluative attitudes of that immediate circle of adults whom the sociol-ogists call his primary group. A boy becomes a man by imi-tating the men around him, and in so doing he irrevocably shapes himself in their image. The way he speaks and carries his body, how he responds to pain or pleasure, the pattern of his behavior toward women, old men, children, the internal psychic economy of his hopes and fears and deepest desires, all are primarily imitative in origin. Throughout life, the individual seeks approval from his "significant others," will-ing to submit even to death rather than violate the mores he has learned. The standards and judgment of his society echo within him as guilt or shame.

Those philosophers are therefore deeply mistaken who suppose that the social inheritance is a burden to be cast off, a spell from which we must be awakened. Without that in-heritance, the individual is exactly nothing—he has no or-ganized core of personality into which his culture has not penetrated. The most thorough radical is the merest reflection of the society against which he rebels. So we are all naturally, irremediably, beneficially, bound up with the social groups in which we locate ourselves and live out our lives.

Since man is by nature an animal that lives in a group, it is folly to set before ourselves as a political ideal a state whose members owe their sole allegiance to the state. A fusion of group loyalty with political obligation is possible only when the primary group is identical with the total society—in short, only in a utopian community like New Lanark or an Israeli kibbutz. In a large society, loyalty to the state must be built upon loyalty to a multiplicity of intra-social groups in which men can find the face-to-face contacts which sustain their personalities and reinforce their value-attitudes.

Morton Grodzins summarizes this theory of "multiple loyalties" in his book, *The Loyal and the Disloyal:*

> The non-national groups, large and small, play a crucial, independent role in the transference of allegiance to the nation. For one thing, they are the means through which citizens are brought to participate in civic affairs and national ceremony. . . . In theory, at least, the chain is an endless one. For if the dictates of government are enforced by the sanctions of the smaller groups, the smaller groups in turn establish the governmental policies they enforce. This is one hallmark of democracy: populations effectuating the policies they determine. Where population groups believe—or understand—this dual role, their patriotic performance is all the stronger. . . . Individuals, in short, act for the nation in response to the smaller groups with which they identify themselves. The larger group, the nation, need only establish the goal. The citizen may or may not participate in this goal definition, may or may not agree with it. Except in rare cases, he will nevertheless sup-

ply the force through which its achievement is at-
tempted. His loyalty to smaller groups insures his
doing it. They perforce must support its causes, especially when, as during war, the very existence of the
nation is at stake. So it is that mothers tearfully send
their unwilling sons to war. So it is that loyalties to
smaller groups supply the guts of national endeavor,
even when that endeavor has no meaning to the individual concerned.   (pp. 65–67)

To each defense of pluralism, there corresponds a defense
of tolerance. In the would-be orthodox society, tolerance of
diversity is a necessary evil, urged by the voices of reason
against the passion of intolerant faith. So the *politiques* of
France avoided a mortal civil war by the Edict of Nantes; so
too modern Russia countenances Titoism in eastern European
territories which it can no longer completely control. Such
tolerance is not a virtue—a strength of the body politic—but a
desperate remedy for a sickness which threatens to be fatal.

To the champion of pluralism as an instrument of democracy, tolerance is the live-and-let-live moderation of the
marketplace. Economic competition is a form of human
struggle (medieval warfare was another) in which each com-
batant simultaneously acknowledges the legitimacy of his op-
ponent's demands and yet gives no quarter in the battle. A
tension exists between implacable opposition on the one hand
and mutual acceptance on the other. If either is lost, the relationship degenerates into cooperation in one case, into unconditional warfare in the other. The capacity to accept competing claims as legitimate is the necessary precondition
of compromise. Insofar as I view my opponents as morally
wrong, compromise becomes appeasement; if my own claims
are unjust, I can press them only out of unwarranted self-
interest. Tolerance in a society of competing interest groups
is precisely the ungrudging acknowledgment of the right of

opposed interests to exist and be pursued. This economic conception of tolerance goes quite naturally with the view of human action as motivated by interests rather than principles or norms. It is much easier to accept a compromise between competing interests—particularly when they are expressible in terms of a numerical scale like money—than between opposed principles which purport to be objectively valid. The genius of American politics is its ability to treat even matters of principle as though they were conflicts of interest. (It has been remarked that the genius of French politics is its ability to treat even conflicts of interest as matters of principle.)

Tolerance plays an even more important role in the third defense of pluralism, the one based upon a group theory of society and personality. In a large society, a multiplicity of groups is essential to the healthy development of the individual, but there is a danger in the emotional commitment which one must make to his primary group. In the jargon of the sociologists, out-group hostility is the natural accompaniment of in-group loyalty. The more warmly a man says "we," the more coldly will he say "they." Out of the individual strength which each draws from his group will come the social weakness of parochial hatred, which is to say, intolerance.

One solution to the problem of intolerance, of course, is to loosen the ties which bind the individual to his ethnic, religious, or economic groups. We are all brothers under the skin, is the message of the humanist; which means the ways in which we are alike matter more than the ways in which we are unlike. But the danger of dissolving parochial loyalties is that without them man cannot live. If the personality needs the reinforcement of immediate response, the face-to-face confirmation of expectations and values, in order to be strong, and if—as this theory claims—no man can truly take a whole nation as his primary group, then it is disastrous to weaken the primary ties even in the name of brotherhood. To do so is to court the evils of "mass man," the unaffiliated, faceless member of the lonely crowd.

The alternative to the indiscriminate leveling of differences in a universal brotherhood is tolerance, a willing acceptance, indeed encouragement, of primary group diversity. If men can be brought to believe that it is positively good for society to contain many faiths, many races, many styles of living, then the healthy consequences of pluralism can be preserved without the sickness of prejudice and civil strife. To draw once again on Plato's way of talking, pluralism is the condition which a modern industrial democracy must possess to function at all; but tolerance is the state of mind which enables it to perform its function well. Hence, on the group theory of society, tolerance is truly the virtue of a pluralist democracy.

II

Thus far, I have simply been expounding the concept of tolerance, exhibiting its place in the theory of democratic pluralism. As we have seen, there are two distinct theories of pluralism, the first emerging from traditional liberal democratic theory and the second from a social-psychological analysis of the group basis of personality and culture. With each is associated a different notion of tolerance. In the first instance, tolerance is equated with the acceptance of individual idiosyncrasy and interpersonal conflict; in the second instance, tolerance is interpreted as the celebration of primary-group diversity. I want now to raise the more difficult question, whether pluralism and tolerance in any of their forms are defensible ideals of democratic society and not simply useful analytical models for describing contemporary America.

The first, or instrumental, theory of pluralism is depend-

ent for its justification on the earlier liberal philosophy from
which it derives. If we wish to evaluate its fundamental
principles, therefore, and not simply its effectiveness as a
means for realizing them, we must go back to the doctrine
of individualism and liberty expressed by John Stuart Mill,
and consider whether it can be defended as an ideal of political society. As we saw in Chapter 1, Mill defends the
sanctity of the individual against what he sees as the unjusti-
fied interference of society and the state. The principle of
utility demands that the private sphere of the individual's
existence be held inviolate, or so Mill argues. But if a liberal
society is to function smoothly, the members of that society
must honor the principle of noninterference cheerfully and
without coercion; otherwise the relations among men will
be characterized by a constant struggle for the assertion and
preservation of private rights. Tolerance, for Mill and classical liberalism, is precisely the readiness of each man to respect the inviolability of the private. A man may choose to
wear strange clothes, grow a beard (or shave one off, if
others wear them), practice unfamiliar religions, deviate
from the sexual norms of his community, or in any other way
reject the tastes and habits of society. The liberal philosophy
demands that society refrain from interfering with his practices, either by legal or by informal social sanctions. What
thus begins as unwilling acceptance of idiosyncrasy may
hopefully flourish as the encouragement of individuality and
the positive enjoyment of diversity.

In his public or other-regarding actions, the individual
is of course held accountable by Mill, but it does not follow
that he must completely bury his personal interests in the
interest of society. Quite to the contrary, society itself, as
the intersection of the public spheres of all the individuals
who make it up, is a marketplace or battleground in which
each individual pursues his private goals to the greatest ex-

tent compatible with the analogous pursuits by others. The only difference is that whereas in the private sector, society has no right at all to interfere with the individual's pursuit, because his actions have no influence upon the lives of others, in the common public sphere society imposes a rule of equity upon its members. Insofar as the mechanism of the marketplace functions efficiently, it will automatically achieve the mutual restrictions and limitations which justice and liberty require. Where the market fails, or in the case of noneconomic matters, the state will step in and legislate the necessary regulation.

If we try to imagine a society in which the ideal of liberal tolerance is achieved in practice, what springs to mind is a large, cosmopolitan, industrial city, such as London or New York or Paris. The size, functional differentiation, speed of movement, fragmentation of social groupings, and density of population all cooperate to create a congenial setting for an attitude of easy tolerance toward diversity of beliefs and practices. It is a commonplace that in the anonymity of the big city one can more easily assemble the precise combination of tastes, habits, and beliefs which satisfy one's personal desires and then find a circle of friends with whom to share them. In the small town or suburb it is impossible to escape from the sort of social interference in private affairs which Mill condemned. But mere size is not sufficient; the true liberation of the individual requires that the city be diverse as well. So the philosophy of tolerance, as expounded by liberalism, leads naturally to an active encouragement of cultural, religious, social, and political variety in an urban setting.

Like all political philosophies, the liberal theory of the state bases itself upon a conception of human nature. In its most primitive form—and it is thus that a philosophy often reveals itself best—liberalism views man as a rationally calculating maximizer of pleasure and minimizer of pain. The term "good," says Bentham, means "pleasant," and the term "bad" means "painful." In all our actions, we seek the first and avoid the second. Rationality thus reduces to a calculating prudence; its highest point is reached when we deliberately shun the present pleasure for fear of the future pain. It is of course a commonplace that this bookkeeping attitude toward sensation is the direct reflection of the bourgeois merchant's attitude toward profit and loss. Equally important, however, is the implication of the theory for the relations between one man and another. If the simple psychological egoism of liberal theory is correct, then each individual must view others as mere instruments in the pursuit of his private ends. As I formulate my desires and weigh the most prudent means for satisfying them, I discover that the actions of other persons, bent upon similar lonely quests, may affect the outcome of my enterprise. In some cases, they threaten me; in others, the possibility exists of a mutually beneficial cooperation. I adjust my plans accordingly, perhaps even entering into quite intricate and enduring alliances with other individuals. But always I seek my own pleasure (or happiness—the shift from one to the other is not of very great significance in liberal theory, although Mill makes much of it). For me, other persons are obstacles to be overcome or resources to be exploited—always means, that is to say, and never ends in themselves. To speak fancifully, it is as though society were an enclosed space in which float a number of spherical balloons filled with an expanding gas. Each balloon increases in size until its surface meets the surface of the other balloons; then it stops growing and adjusts to its surroundings. Justice in such a society could only mean the protection of each balloon's interior (Mill's private sphere) and the equal apportionment of space to all. What took place within an individual would be no business of the others.*

In the more sophisticated versions of liberal philosophy, the crude picture of man as a pleasure maximizer is softened somewhat. Mill recognizes that men may pursue higher ends than pleasure, at least as that feeling or sensation is usually understood, and he even recognizes the possibility of altruistic or other-regarding feelings of sympathy and compassion. Nevertheless, society continues to be viewed as a system of independent centers of consciousness, each pursuing its own gratification and confronting the others as beings standing-over-against the self, which is to say, as *objects*. The condition of the individual in such a state of affairs is what a different tradition of social philosophy would call "alienation."

Dialectically opposed to the liberal philosophy and speaking for the values of an earlier, preindustrial, age is the conservative philosophy of community. The involvement of each with all, which to Mill was a threat and an imposition, is to such critics of liberalism as Burke or Durkheim a strength and an opportunity. It is indeed the greatest virtue of society, which supports and enfolds the individual in a warm, affective community stretching backwards and forwards in time and bearing within itself the accumulated wisdom and values of generations of human experience.

The fundamental insight of the conservative philosophy is that man is by nature a social being. This is not simply to say that he is gregarious, that he enjoys the company of his fellows, although that is true of man, as it is also of monkeys and otters. Rather, man is social in the sense that his essence, his true being, lies in his involvement in a human community. Aristotle, in the opening pages of the *Politics*, says that

---

* For a more detailed analysis of this doctrine, and an alternative to it, see Chapter 5 below.

man is by nature a being intended to live in a political community. Those men who, by choice, live outside such a community are, he says, either lower or higher than other men—that is, either animals or angels. Now man is like the animals in respect of his bodily desires, and he is like the angels in respect of his reason. In a sense, therefore, liberalism has made the mistake of supposing that man is no more than a combination of the bestial and the angelic, the passionate and the rational. From such an assumption it follows naturally that man, like both beasts and angels, is essentially a lonely creature.

But, Aristotle tells us, man has a mode of existence peculiar to his species, based on the specifically human faculty for communication. That mode of existence is society, which is a human community bound together by rational discourse and shared values. Prudence and passion combine to make a rational pleasure calculator, but they do not make a man.

The conservative figure whose work contrasts most sharply with Mill's is the French sociologist Emile Durkheim. In a seminal study of social integration entitled *Suicide,* Durkheim undertook to expose the foundations of the individual's involvement with his society by examining the conditions under which that involvement broke down in the most dramatic way. Durkheim discovered that proneness to suicide was associated, in contemporary western society, with one of two sorts of conditions, both of which are parts of what Mill calls "liberty." The loosening of the constraints of traditional and group values creates in some individuals a condition of lawlessness, an absence of limits on desire and ambition. Since there is no intrinsic limit to the quantity of satisfaction which the self can seek, it finds itself drawn into an endless and frustrating pursuit of pleasure. The infinitude of the objective universe is unconstrained for the individual within social or subjective limits, and the self is simply dissipated in the vacuum which it strives to fill. When this lack of internal limitation saps the strength and organization of the personality beyond bearable limits, suicide is liable to result; Durkheim labels this form of suicide "anomic" in order to indicate the lawlessness which causes it.

Freedom from the constraint of traditional and social values brings with it a loss of limits and the abyss of anomie, according to Durkheim. (Note that the term "anomie," as originally defined by Durkheim, does *not* mean loneliness, loss of a sense of identity, or anonymity in a mass. It means quite precisely a-nomie, or lack of law.) Freedom from the constricting bonds of an intimate social involvement brings with it a second form of psychic derangement, called by Durkheim "egoism," which also leads in extreme cases to suicide. Durkheim sees the human condition as inherently tragic. The individual is launched upon an infinite expanse, condemned to seek a security which must always pass away in death and to project meaning into a valueless void. The only hope is for men to huddle together and collectively create the warm world of meaning and coherence which impersonal nature cannot offer. Each of us sees himself reflected in the other selves of his society, and together we manage to forget for a time the reality beyond the walls. Erik Erikson captures this sense of the besieged community in his discussion of the Russian character, in *Childhood and Society*. Erikson is portraying the traditional Russian peasant community as it appears in the opening scenes of a moving picture of Maxim Gorky's youth. Erikson writes:

> At the beginning there is the Russian trinity: empty plains, Volga, balalaika. The vast horizons of central Russia reveal their vast emptinesses; and immediately balalaika tunes rise to compassionate crescendos, as if they were saying, "You are not alone, we are all here." Somewhere along the Volga broad river boats deliver

bundled-up people into isolated villages and crowded towns.

The vastness of the land and the refuge of the small, gay community thus are the initial theme. One is reminded of the fact that "mir," the word for village, also means world, and of the saying, "Even death is good if you are in the mir." A thousand years ago the Vikings called the Russians "the people of the stockades" because they had found them huddling together in their compact towns, thus surviving winters, beasts, and invaders—and enjoying themselves in their own rough ways. (p. 318)

Durkheim marshals statistics to show that where the intensity of the collective life of a community diminishes—as their "freedom," in Mill's sense, increases, therefore—the rate of suicide rises. Thus Protestant communities exhibit higher rates than Catholic communities, which in turn surpass the inward-turning Jewish communities. So too, education is "positively" correlated with suicide, for although knowledge in itself is not harmful to the human personality, the independence of group norms and isolation which higher education carries with it quite definitely is inimical. One might almost see in the varying suicide rates a warning which society issues to those of its number who foolishly venture past the walls of the town into the limitless and lonely wastes beyond.

It seems, if Durkheim is correct, that the very liberty and individuality which Mill celebrates are deadly threats to the integrity and health of the personality. So far from being superfluous constraints which thwart the free development of the self, social norms protect us from the dangers of anomie; and that invasive intimacy of each with each which Mill felt as suffocating is actually our principal protection against the soul-destroying evil of isolation.

Needless to say, the dark vision of Durkheim was not shared by all of the conservative critics of liberal society, though more often than not the inexorable advance of industrialism provoked in them an extreme pessimism. In those who wrote early in the century or even at the close of the eighteenth century, there still lived a hope that the traditional society of the preceding age could be preserved. So we find Burke singing the praises of the continuing community of values and institutions which was England and damning the French revolution as an anarchic and destructive deviation which could hopefully be corrected. Whether the critics of liberalism saw its advance as inevitable or as reversible, the more perceptive among them recognized in its espousal of tolerance the principal threat to the traditional society of shared values and communal integration. The very essence of social constraint is that one feels it as objective, external, unavoidable, and hence genuinely a limit beyond which one's desires may not extend. As soon as one enunciates the doctrine of the liberty of the internal life, those constraints become no more than suggestions—or, when backed by force, threats. But the individual is not capable of the self-regulation which Mill's doctrine of liberty presupposes. He is like a little child who ventures forth bravely to explore the playground but looks back every few moments to reassure himself that his mother is still there. So, we might say, evoking the images of traditional society, the adult ventures forth to explore life, secure in the knowledge that mother church and a paternal monarch will guide and support him. The recurrent use of familial metaphors in the description of social institutions expresses the dependent relationship which all men bear to their human community. Mill assures us in a number of passages that his principles of individual liberty are not meant to apply to children, who of course are not yet ready to assume the burden of freedom. What he fails to grasp, his conservative opponents seem to be telling us, is that men are the children of their societies throughout their lives. Absolute tolerance therefore has the same disastrous effects on the adult personality as extreme permissiveness on the growing child. In that sense, "progressive" theories of child-rearing are the true reflections of the liberal philosophy.

In the conflict between liberalism and conservatism, neither side can claim a monopoly of valid arguments or legitimate insights. The liberal apologists are surely correct in seeing traditional constraints as fetters which prevent the full development of human potentialities and tie men to unjust patterns of domination. What is more, the liberals at least are prepared to accept the burden of lost innocence which men bear in the modern age. To embrace traditions after their authority has been undermined is to retreat into an antiquarian refuge. It is absurd to decide *on rational grounds* that one will accept nonrational authority. There can be no turning back from the "liberation" of modern society, whatever one thinks of its desirability.

At the same time, the liberal assurance that the burdens of freedom can easily be borne is contradicted by the facts of contemporary life, as the conservative sociologists so clearly perceived. The elimination of superstition, on which the eighteenth-century *philosophes* counted so heavily, and the liberation from social constraints for which Mill had such hopes are at best ambiguous accomplishments. The problem which forces itself upon the unillusioned supporter of liberal principles is to formulate a social philosophy which achieves some consistency between the ideals of justice and individual freedom on the one hand and the facts of the social origin and nature of personality on the other. Durk-

heim himself rejected any easy nostalgia for the communal
glories of a past age. After demonstrating the correlation
between education and suicide, he warned:

> Far from knowledge being the source of the evil, it is
> its remedy, the only remedy we have. Once established
> beliefs have been carried away by the current of affairs,
> they cannot be artificially reestablished; only reflection
> can guide us in life, after this. Once the social instinct is
> blunted, intelligence is the only guide left us and we
> have to reconstruct a conscience by its means. Danger-
> ous as is the undertaking there can be no hesitation, for
> we have no choice. Let those who view anxiously and
> sadly the ruins of ancient beliefs, who feel all the diffi-
> culties of these critical times, not ascribe to science an
> evil it has not caused but rather which it tries to
> cure! . . . The authority of vanished traditions will
> never be restored by silencing it; we shall only be more
> powerless to replace them. . . . If minds cannot be
> made to lose the desire for freedom by artificially en-
> slaving them, neither can they recover their equilibrium
> by mere freedom. They must use this freedom fittingly.
>   (p. 169)

Democratic pluralism, as it developed in the context of
American life and politics during the late nineteenth and
early twentieth century, purports to achieve just the required union of "liberal" principles and "conservative" sociology. As we saw in the first part of this chapter, pluralism
espouses a tolerance and noninterference in the private
sphere which are precisely analogous to the classical liberal
doctrine; however, the units of society between which tolerance and mutual acceptance are to be exercised are not
isolated individuals but human groups, specifically religious,
ethnic, and racial groups. All the arguments which Mill advanced in defense of the individual's right to differ from the

surrounding society are taken over in pluralistic democracy as arguments for the right of a social group to differ from other social groups. At the same time, it is assumed that the individual will belong to some group or other—which is to say, that he will identify with and internalize the values of an existing infra-national community. We thus can see the implicit rationale for what is otherwise a most peculiar characteristic of pluralistic democracy, namely the combination of tolerance for the most diverse social groups and extreme intolerance for the idiosyncratic individual. One might expect, for example, that a society which urges its citizens to "attend the church or synagogue of your choice" would be undismayed by an individual who chose to attend no religious service at all. Similarly, it would seem natural—at least on traditional principles of individual liberty—to extend to the bearded and be-sandaled "beat" the same generous tolerance which Americans are accustomed to grant to the Amish, or orthodox Jews, or any other groups whose dress and manner deviate from the norm. Instead, we find a strange mixture of the greatest tolerance for what we might call established groups and an equally great intolerance for the deviant individual. The justification for this attitude, which would be straightforwardly contradictory on traditional liberal grounds, is the doctrine of pluralistic democracy. If it is good for each individual to conform to some social group and good as well that a diversity of social groups be welcomed in the community at large, then one can consistently urge group tolerance and individual intolerance.

On this analysis, the "conservative liberalism" of contemporary American politics is more than merely a ritual preference for the middle of any road. It is a coherent social philosophy which combines the ideals of classical liberalism with the psychological and political realities of modern plu-

ralistic society. In America, this hybrid doctrine serves a
number of social purposes simultaneously, as I tried to indicate in my preliminary discussion of the origins of pluralism.
It eases the conflicts among antagonistic groups of immigrants, achieves a working harmony among the several great
religions, diminishes the intensity of regional oppositions,
and integrates the whole into the hierarchical federal political structure inherited from the founding fathers, while at
the same time encouraging and preserving the psychologically desirable forces of social integration which traditional
liberalism tended to weaken.

III

Democratic pluralism and its attendant principle of tolerance
are considerably more defensible than either of the traditions
out of which they grow; nevertheless, they are open to a
number of serious criticisms which are, in my opinion, ultimately fatal to pluralism as a defensible ideal of social
policy. The weaknesses of pluralism lie not so much in its
theoretical formulation as in the covert ideological consequences of its application to the reality of contemporary
America. The sense of "ideological" which I intend is that
adopted by Karl Mannheim in his classic study *Ideology and
Utopia*. Mannheim defines ideology as follows:

> The concept "ideology" reflects the one discovery which
> emerged from political conflict, namely, that ruling
> groups can in their thinking become so intensively
> interest-bound to a situation that they are simply no
> longer able to see certain facts which would undermine
> their sense of domination. There is implicit in the word
> "ideology" the insight that in certain situations the
> collective unconscious of certain groups obscures the
> real condition of society both to itself and to others and
> thereby stabilizes it.   (p. 40)

Ideology is thus systematically self-serving thought, in two senses. First, and most simply, it is the refusal to recognize unpleasant facts which might require a less flattering evaluation of a policy or institution or which might undermine one's claim to a right of domination. For example, slave-owners in the antebellum South refused to acknowledge that the slaves themselves were unhappy. The implication was that if they were, then slavery would be harder to justify. Secondly, ideological thinking is a denial of unsettling or revolutionary factors in society on the principle of the self-confirming prophecy that the more stable everyone believes the situation to be, the more stable it actually becomes.

One might think that whatever faults the theory of pluralism possessed, at least it would be free of the dangers of ideological distortion. Does it not accord a legitimate place to all groups in society? How then can it be used to justify or preserve the dominance of one group over another? In fact, I shall try to show that the application of pluralist theory to American society involves ideological distortion in at least three different ways. The first stems from the "vector-sum" or "balance-of-power" interpretation of pluralism; the second arises from the application of the "referee" version of the theory; and the third is inherent in the abstract theory itself.

According to the vector-sum theory of pluralism, the major groups in society compete through the electoral process for control over the actions of the government. Politicians are forced to accommodate themselves to a number of opposed interests and in so doing achieve a rough distributive justice. What are the major groups which, according to pluralism, comprise American society today? First, there are the hereditary groups which are summarized by that catch-phrase of tolerance, "without regard to race, creed, color, or national origin." In addition there are the major economic interest groups among which—so the theory goes, a healthy balance is maintained: labor, business, agriculture, and—a residual category, this—the consumer. Finally, there are a number of voluntary associations whose size, permanence, and influence entitle them to a place in any group-analysis of America, groups such as the veterans' organizations and the American Medical Association.

At one time, this may have been an accurate account of American society. But once constructed, the picture becomes frozen, and when changes take place in the patterns of social or economic grouping, they tend not to be acknowledged because they deviate from that picture. So the application of the theory of pluralism always favors the groups in existence against those in process of formation. For example, at any given time the major religious, racial, and ethnic groups are viewed as permanent and exhaustive categories into which every American can conveniently be pigeonholed. Individuals who fall outside any major social group—the non-religious, say—are treated as exceptions and relegated in practice to a second-class status. Thus agnostic conscientious objectors are required to serve in the armed forces, while those who claim even the most bizarre religious basis for their refusal are treated with ritual tolerance and excused by the courts. Similarly, orphanages in America are so completely dominated by the three major faiths that a non-religious or religiously mixed couple simply cannot adopt a child in many states. The net effect is to preserve the official three-great-religions image of American society long after it has ceased to correspond to social reality and to discourage individuals from officially breaking their religious ties. A revealing example of the mechanism of tolerance is the ubiquitous joke about "the priest, the minister, and the rabbi." A world of insight into the psychology of tolerance can be had simply from observing the mixture of emotions with which an audience greets such a joke, as told by George Jessel or some other apostle of "interfaith understanding." One senses embarrassment, nervousness, and finally an explosion of self-congratulatory laughter as though everyone were relieved at a difficult moment got through without incident. The gentle ribbing nicely distributed in the story among the three men of the cloth gives each member of the audience a chance to express his hostility safely and acceptably, and in the end to reaffirm the principle of tolerance by joining in the applause. Only a bigot, one feels, could refuse to crack a smile!

Rather more serious in its conservative falsifying of social reality is the established image of the major economic groups of American society. The emergence of a rough parity between big industry and organized labor has been paralleled by the rise of a philosophy of moderation and cooperation between them, based on mutual understanding and respect, which is precisely similar to the achievement of interfaith and ethnic tolerance. What has been overlooked or suppressed is the fact that there are tens of millions of Americans—businessmen and workers alike—whose interests are completely ignored by this genial give-and-take. Nonunionized workers are worse off after each price-wage increase, as are the thousands of small businessmen who cannot survive in the competition against great nationwide firms. The theory of pluralism does not espouse the interests of the unionized against the nonunionized, or of large against small business; but by presenting a picture of the American economy in which those disadvantaged elements do not appear, it tends to perpetuate the inequality by ignoring rather than justifying it.

The case here is the same as with much ideological thinking. Once pluralists acknowledge the existence of groups whose interests are not weighed in the labor-business balance, then their own theory requires them to call for an alteration of the system. If migrant workers, or white-collar workers, or small businessmen are genuine *groups,* then they have a legitimate place in the system of group-adjustments. Thus, pluralism is not explicitly a philosophy of privilege or injustice—it is a philosophy of equality and justice whose *concrete application* supports inequality by ignoring the existence of certain legitimate social groups.

This ideological function of pluralism helps to explain one of the peculiarities of American politics. There is a very sharp distinction in the public domain between legitimate interests and those which are absolutely beyond the pale. If a group or interest is within the framework of acceptability, then it can be sure of winning some measure of what it seeks, for the process of national politics is distributive and compromising. On the other hand, if an interest falls *outside* the circle of the acceptable, it receives no attention whatsoever and its proponents are treated as crackpots, extremists, or foreign agents. With bewildering speed, an interest can move from "outside" to "inside" and its partisans, who have been scorned by the solid and established in the community, become presidential advisers and newspaper columnists.

A vivid example from recent political history is the sudden legitimation of the problem of poverty in America. In the postwar years, tens of millions of poor Americans were left behind by the sustained growth of the economy. The facts were known and discussed for years by fringe critics whose attempts to call attention to these forgotten Americans were greeted with either silence or contempt. Suddenly, poverty was "discovered" by Presidents Kennedy and Johnson, and articles were published in *Look* and *Time* which a year earlier would have been more at home in the radical journals which inhabit political limbo in America. A social group whose very existence had long been denied was now the object of a national crusade.

A similar elevation from obscurity to relative prominence was experienced by the peace movement, a "group" of a rather different nature. For years, the partisans of disarmament labored to gain a hearing for their view that nuclear war could not be a reasonable instrument of national policy. Sober politicians and serious columnists treated such ideas as the naive fantasies of bearded peaceniks, communist sympathizers, and well-meaning but hopelessly muddled clerics. Then suddenly the Soviet Union achieved the nuclear parity which had been long forecast, the prospect of which had convinced disarmers of the insanity of nuclear war. Sober reevaluations appeared in the columns of Walter Lippmann, and some even found their way into the speeches of President Kennedy—what had been unthinkable, absurd, naive, dangerous, even subversive, six months before, was now plausible, sound, thoughtful, and—within another six months —official American policy.

The explanation for these rapid shifts in the political winds lies, I suggest, in the logic of pluralism. According to pluralist theory, every genuine social group has a right to a voice in the making of policy and a share in the benefits. Any policy urged by a group in the system must be given respectful attention, no matter how bizarre. By the same token, a policy or principle which lacks legitimate representation has no place in the society, no matter how reasonable or right it may be. Consequently, the line between acceptable and unacceptable alternatives is very sharp, so that the territory of American politics is like a plateau with steep cliffs on all sides rather than like a pyramid. On the plateau are all the interest groups which are recognized as legitimate; in the deep valley all around lie the outsiders, the fringe groups which are scorned as "extremist." The most important battle waged by any group in American politics is the struggle to climb onto the plateau. Once there, it can count on some measure of what it seeks. No group ever gets all of what it wants, and no *legitimate* group is completely frustrated in its efforts.

Thus, the "vector-sum" version of pluralist theory functions ideologically by tending to deny new groups or interests access to the political plateau. It does this by ignoring their existence in practice, not by denying their claim in theory. The result is that pluralism has a braking effect on social change; it slows down transformation in the system of group adjustments but does not set up an absolute barrier to change. For this reason, as well as because of its origins as a fusion of two conflicting social philosophies, it deserves the title "conservative liberalism."

According to the second, or "referee," version of pluralism, the role of the government is to oversee and regulate the competition among interest groups in the society. Out of the applications of this theory have grown not only countless laws, such as the antitrust bills, pure food and drug acts, and Taft-Hartley Law, but also the complex system of quasi-judicial regulatory agencies in the executive branch of government. Henry Kariel, in a powerful and convincing book entitled *The Decline of American Pluralism*, has shown that this referee function of government, as it actually works out in practice, systematically favors the interests of the stronger against the weaker party in interest-group conflicts and tends to solidify the power of those who already hold it. The government, therefore, plays a conservative, rather than a neutral, role in the society.

Kariel details the ways in which this discriminatory influence is exercised. In the field of regulation of labor unions, for example, the federal agencies deal with the established leadership of the unions. In such matters as the overseeing of union elections, the settlement of jurisdictional disputes, or the setting up of mediation boards, it is the interests of those leaders rather than the competing interests of rank-and-file dissidents which are favored. In the regulation of agriculture, again, the locally most influential farmers or leaders of farmers' organizations draw up the guidelines for control which are then adopted by the federal inspectors. In each case, ironically, the unwillingness of the government to impose its own standards or rules results not in a free play of competing groups, but in the enforcement of the preferences of the existing predominant interests.

In a sense, these unhappy consequences of government regulation stem from a confusion between a theory of interest-conflict and a theory of power-conflict. The government quite successfully referees the conflict among competing *powers*—any group which has already managed to accumulate a significant quantum of power will find its claims attended to by the federal agencies. But legitimate *interests* which have been ignored, suppressed, defeated, or which have not yet succeeded in organizing themselves for effective action, will find their disadvantageous position perpetuated through the decisions of the government. It is as though an umpire were to come upon a baseball game in progress between big boys and little boys, in which the big boys cheated, broke the rules, claimed hits that were outs, and made the little boys accept the injustice by brute force. If the umpire undertakes to "regulate" the game by simply enforcing the "rules" actually being practiced, he does not thereby make the game a fair one. Indeed, he may actually make matters worse, because if the little boys get up their courage, band together, and decide to fight it out, the umpire will accuse them of breaking the rules and throw his weight against them! Precisely the same sort of thing happens in pluralist politics. For example, the American Medical Association exercises a stranglehold over American medicine through its influence over the government's licensing regulations. Doctors who are opposed to the A.M.A.'s political positions, or even to its medical policies, do not merely have to buck the entrenched authority of the organization's leaders. They must also risk the loss of hospital affiliations, speciality accreditation, and so forth, all of which powers have been placed in the hands of the medical establishment by state and federal laws. Those laws are written by the government in cooperation with the very same A.M.A. leaders; not surprisingly, the interests of dissenting doctors do not receive favorable attention.

The net effect of government action is thus to weaken, rather than strengthen, the play of conflicting interests in the society. The theory of pluralism here has a crippling effect upon the government, for it warns against positive federal intervention in the name of independent principles of justice, equality, or fairness. The theory says justice will emerge from the free interplay of opposed groups; the practice tends to destroy that interplay.

Finally, the theory of pluralism in all its forms has the effect in American thought and politics of discriminating not only against certain social groups or interests, but also against certain sorts of proposals for the solution of social problems. According to pluralist theory, politics is a contest among social groups for control of the power and decision of the government. Each group is motivated by some interest or cluster of interests and seeks to sway the government toward action in its favor. The typical social problem according to pluralism is therefore some instance of distributive injustice. One group is getting too much, another too little, of the available resources. In accord with its modification of traditional liberalism, pluralism's goal is a rough parity among competing groups rather than among competing individuals. Characteristically, new proposals originate with a group which feels that its legitimate interests have been slighted, and the legislative outcome is a measure which corrects the social imbalance to a degree commensurate with the size and political power of the initiating group.

But there are some social ills in America whose causes do not lie in a maldistribution of wealth, and which cannot be cured therefore by the techniques of pluralist politics. For example, America is growing uglier, more dangerous, and less pleasant to live in, as its citizens grow richer. The reason is that natural beauty, public order, the cultivation of the arts, are not the special interest of any identifiable social group. Consequently, evils and inadequacies in those areas cannot be remedied by shifting the distribution of wealth and power among existing social groups. To be sure, crime and urban slums hurt the poor more than the rich, the Negro more than the white—but fundamentally they are problems of the society as a whole, not of any particular group. That is to say, they concern the general good, not merely the aggregate of private goods. To deal with such problems, there must be some way of constituting the whole society a genuine group with a group purpose and a conception of the common good. Pluralism rules this out in theory by portraying society as an aggregate of human communities rather than as itself a human community; and it equally rules out a concern for the general good in practice by encouraging a politics of interest-group pressures in which there is no mechanism for the discovery and expression of the common good.

The theory and practice of pluralism first came to dominate American politics during the depression, when the Democratic party put together an electoral majority of minority groups. It is not at all surprising that the same period saw the demise of an active socialist movement, for socialism, both in its diagnosis of the ills of industrial capitalism and in its proposed remedies, focuses on the structure of the economy and society as a whole and advances programs in the name of the general good. Pluralism, both as theory and as practice, simply does not acknowledge the possibility of wholesale reorganization of the society. By insisting on the group nature of society, it denies the existence of society-wide interests—save the purely procedural interest in preserving the system of group pressures—and the possibility of communal action in pursuit of the general good.

A proof of this charge can be found in the commissions, committees, institutes, and conferences which are convened from time to time to ponder the "national interest." The membership of these assemblies always includes an enlightened business executive, a labor leader, an educator, several clergymen of various faiths, a woman, a literate general or admiral, and a few public figures of unquestioned sobriety and predictable views. The whole is a microcosm of the interest groups and hereditary groups which, according to pluralism, constitute American society. Any vision of the national interest which emerges from such a group will inevitably be a standard pluralist picture of a harmonious, cooperative, distributively just, *tolerant* America. One could hardly expect a committee of group representatives to decide that the pluralist system of social groups is an obstacle to the general good!

IV

Pluralist democracy, with its virtue, tolerance, constitutes the highest stage in the political development of industrial capitalism. It transcends the crude "limitations" of early individualistic liberalism and makes a place for the communitarian features of social life, as well as for the interest-group politics which emerged as a domesticated version of the class struggle. Pluralism is humane, benevolent, accommodating, and far more responsive to the evils of social injustice than either the egoistic liberalism or the traditionalistic conservatism from which it grew. But pluralism is fatally blind to the evils which afflict the entire body politic, and as a theory of society it obstructs consideration of precisely the sorts of thoroughgoing social revisions which may be needed to remedy those evils. Like all great social theories, pluralism answered a genuine social need during a significant period of history. Now, however, new problems confront America, problems not of distributive injustice but of the common good. We must give up the image of society as a battleground of competing groups and formulate an ideal of society more exalted than the mere acceptance of opposed interests and diverse customs. There is need for a new philosophy of community. In the final chapter, we shall take a first step toward the formulation of that philosophy.

5. Community

THUS FAR, the thrust of this book has been almost entirely critical. In the first four chapters, I have tried to develop two interrelated theses: First, that serious conceptual confusion is produced by the attempt to superimpose a collectivist sociology on an individualist liberal political philosophy; and Second, that this unhappy combination frequently serves the conservative ideological purpose of defending existing institutions and limiting the scope of social criticism. Some readers will simply reject these two theses as untrue, or at least as unproven by the arguments presented in the discussions of liberty, loyalty, power, and tolerance. But even those sympathetic readers who find some merit in the arguments may by now feel, rather restively, that a purely negative critique is little better than no critique at all. Even granting that there is a conflict between the individualistic presuppositions of the tradition of political liberalism and the collectivist methodology of sociology and social psychology, how is the conflict to be resolved? Were this a European treatise, I could perhaps close my discussion gracefully with a few words about the need for a dialectical synthesis of individualism and collectivism, but I fear that would hardly satisfy a more analytically trained American audience. Nor is there much to be gained from breathing the magic word "socialism," as though once the password had been pronounced the gates of the City of Man would forthwith swing wide. It may well be, as I tried to suggest in the chapter on Power, that an advance in the rational solution of existing social problems requires an extension of collective social control to areas of social life which are not now objects of decisions. But such an extension does not *resolve* the conflict with the individualist principles of liberalism; it merely poses it anew.

Unfortunately, I cannot conclude this book with the systematic exposition of a new social philosophy which resolves the conflicts I have been exploring.* Nevertheless, in this final essay I wish to take one step forward by analyzing and explicating the concept which, I am convinced, must serve as the key to a new social philosophy, namely the concept of *community*. I use the term "community" because in English it rather conveniently signifies both a certain kind of social group and also the property or characteristic possessed by that group. A number of other terms have been used in discussions of social philosophy for roughly the same idea, including "public interest," "general good," "common good," and "common interest." My aim is not to dissect the subtle variations in usage which have attached to these terms, but instead to get at the important notion which they all seek to capture.

I

As soon as we turn our attention to the notion of the *general good*, the *public interest*, or the *community* of a society, we encounter a very peculiar problem: A great many social

* The problem is a limitation of ideas, not of space!

philosophers flatly deny that those terms refer to anything at all, actual or possible, good or bad, desirable or undesirable. If we can draw a religious analogy, the dispute between proponents and opponents of the general good is akin to the dispute between believers and atheists, rather than that between worshippers of different gods. One side says that there is such a thing as the general good, which we all ought to pursue, and the other side says that the words "general good," if they are not taken merely to refer to some aggregate of private goods, are a meaningless phrase to which nothing could possibly correspond.

Disputes of this sort are common in the history of philosophy. The greatest of them, of course, is the one just mentioned over the concept of God. When Hume and Kant killed rational theology in the eighteenth century, they did so not by proving that there is no God, but by showing that the very concept of God was confused and incoherent. It turned out to be, in a very complicated way, rather like the concept of a round square or a four-sided triangle. Those same two philosophers disagreed about the legitimacy of another concept on which science rather than religion was based, namely the concept of causation. Hume's criticisms of the concept of cause and effect were so powerful that Kant invented a whole new kind of philosophical argument to meet them. Drawing on German legal terminology, he coined the term "deduction." He meant by this not a syllogistic derivation, but rather an argument which establishes the credentials of a concept by showing that it is genuinely coherent and hence has a *possible* application.

In this essay, I am going to offer a deduction, in the Kantian sense, of the concept of community. Since this type of argument is even now unfamiliar outside philosophical circles, let me spend a few brief paragraphs explaining how it works. Suppose that I were invited to go on a griffin hunt.

Not knowing what a griffin is, I would ask the hunt leader to tell me what I was to look for, and he would reply that I must keep a sharp eye out for a huge beast with the head and wings of an eagle and the body and hind quarters of a lion. Now, I might have my doubts about the probability of encountering such a creature, but at least I would know what to look for, and I would most certainly recognize one if I found it. The concept of a griffin, in other words, is a legitimate *concept*, even if there is nothing actually corresponding to it in the world, because I can specify the criteria I would apply to anything in order to determine whether it is a griffin. To put the point negatively, I cannot tell merely from the concept of a griffin that there aren't any. I must appeal to actual experience of the world to settle the matter, and even then I can only be reasonably sure, not absolutely certain. After all, somewhere in the vastness of space there may be a planet on which eagle-headed lions roam.

But now suppose a sociologist friend were to show me his application for a government grant to do a statistical study of the incidence of married bachelors in the American population, with special attention to the relation between religious affiliation and married bachelorhood. Without ever leaving my armchair, I could confidently assure him that he would never find a married bachelor, Protestant, Catholic, or Jew! The point is, of course, that "married bachelor" is a contradiction in terms. The criteria for being married precisely conflict with the criteria for being a bachelor, so that nothing logically *could* meet both sets of criteria at once. Even on a planet of eagle-headed lions there will not be any married bachelors.

Ever since Plato grounded his political philosophy in a questionable analogy between the parts of the soul and the classes of society, social philosophers have played on the metaphor of the state as man writ large. "The body politic," "the health of the state," and all the other familiar phrases imply that we can view society or the state as though it were a quasi-person, with desires, needs, volition, and interests of its own. In the hands of some Idealist philosophers of the nineteenth century, this shaky analogy became an argument for subordinating the good of individuals to some mysterious "general good" or "good of the state," which of course most often turned out to be the interest of those who controlled the instruments of domination.

Liberal political philosophers have responded to those totalitarian tendencies by arguing, on methodologically individualist grounds, that the notion of the state as an organic entity is inherently confused. They insist that there is simply no sense to be found in the concept of a general good or public interest which transcends private goods or interests and stands in contrast to them as an appropriate ideal of social action. The following statement from David Truman's *The Governmental Process*, expresses this point of view well:

> There is a political significance in assertions of a totally inclusive interest within a nation. Particularly in times of crisis, such as an international war, such claims are a tremendously useful promotional device by means of which a particularly extensive group or league of groups tries to reduce or eliminate opposing interests . . . Assertion of an inclusive "national" or "public interest" is an effective device in many less critical situations as well. In themselves, these claims are part of the data of politics. However, they do not describe any actual or possible political situation within a complex modern nation. In developing a group interpretation of politics, therefore, we do not need to account for a totally inclusive interest, because one does not exist. (pp. 50–51)

Even if I can show that there is a legitimate distinction to be made between private interests and the public interest, or private goods and the general good, I shall still be a long way from stating or defending a new social philosophy. It is one thing, after all, to demonstrate that the phrase "general good" has a legitimate, coherent usage, and quite another to show that a society ought to choose the general good as its goal. In this essay, I claim only to provide the "deduction" which must precede any systematic elaboration of a philosophy of community, but my discussion has two subsidiary aims which, if successful, should carry the subject a good deal further forward: First, I shall connect up the concepts of community and public interest with the conservative and radical attacks on nineteenth-century liberalism; and Second, I shall sketch the three modes of community—affective community, community of labor, and rational community—which I believe to be the content of the true general good. Although I do not have a systematic proof of the objective goodness of these three forms of community, I hope that when their precise nature is made clear, they will commend themselves to the reader as an appealing alternative to modern liberalism's ideals of private satisfaction and public justice.

II

Men are by nature purposive beings. Their action is goal-oriented and their practical reasoning concerns both the proper ends of action and the appropriate means for achieving those ends. An action, as opposed merely to a bodily movement, is a bit of behavior which is motivated and guided by the idea of some end or purpose. Frequently, of course, men choose their ends unwisely, but insofar as they can truly be said to *act*, they always have ends.

In their choices of ends, men are inclined by their attitudes, both positive and negative, toward the objects, acts, experiences, and states of affairs which might possibly serve as their goals. Men desire, yearn, love, want, hope, need, aspire; they hate, shun, deprecate, abhor, reject. Insofar as a man adopts an attitude toward some object or state of affairs which does, or might, motivate him to act for it or against it, we may say that he *takes an interest in* it. Generally speaking, interests can be classified as pro- or con-, although that fact is no part of our argument. Taking the term "interest" in its widest possible sense, even at the price of precision in definition, we may say that interest is the characteristic orientation of men toward the world insofar as they are active, rather than merely contemplative.

Following the terminology adopted by the American philosopher Ralph Barton Perry, I propose to define "a value" as "any object of any interest." Whatever anyone actually takes an interest of any sort in, will be called *a value*. Since men take negative as well as positive interests in things, we can speak of positive and negative values.

Everything which could be the object of someone's interest will be labeled a *possible* value. Since the range of objects or states of affairs which someone or other logically could wish to bring into existence or eliminate from existence is rather wide, the class of "possible values" will be a broad one. Men might, for example, want to produce pleasant states of consciousness; they might also want to produce unpleasant states of consciousness (in themselves or others). They might want to build bridges, level mountains, achieve peace on earth, or get into heaven. All of these then are possible values. If a man wishes to win a race, then *winning the race* is the object of his interest, and hence for him "a" value. Only those things which could not even possibly be goals of action are excluded as possible values. For example, it is logically impossible to attempt to bring into being the number seven, so the number seven is *not* a possible value.

Clearly the term "value," as I have defined it, is value-neutral! That is to say, it is a *descriptive* rather than an evaluative term. To say that X is a value is simply to say that somewhere, someone takes a positive or negative interest in it. To say of anything that it *could be* a value is to say that someone *could* take an interest in it. Since there is almost certainly *some* madman around who wishes the world to come to an end and who would bring on Apocalypse if he could, we may confidently assert that the end of the world is at present a value. Since there are also, thank heavens, some people who seek to avoid the end of the world, it is also true that the continuation of the world is at present a value.

The term "value" is inherently dangerous, and I have committed myself to it only because no other term seems as convenient. For example, the use of "value" which I am adopting implies *nothing whatsoever* about the wisdom, prudence, or moral justification of men's interests. It is perfectly possible that no one *ever* adopts the appropriate attitudes toward objects, and it is certain that most men have foolish or immoral interests at least part of the time. So when I say that some object or state of affairs *is a value,* it must not be thought that I am covertly saying that it *has value,* in the sense of being a *worthy* object of interest. Unfortunately, it is a dead certainty that someone reading these lines will attribute that view to me. I only hope that these cautionary remarks will reduce the frequency of such misreadings.*

There are a number of familiar ways of classifying possible values. We may, for example, distinguish instrumental

---

* The purpose of this essay, it should be recalled, is to show that there is a *possible* goal of social action corresponding to the frequently used words "public good" or "general good." In other words, I shall try to prove that the general good is a *possible value.* For this purpose, it would be disastrous to define the term "value" in such a way that it carried a covert evaluative significance. Once we have shown that the general good is a *possible* object of social action, then we can try to find arguments to show that it is a *worthy* object of social action. The two propositions are quite distinct.

from intrinsic values, or economic, aesthetic, religious, and moral values, or simple and complex values, or values which are objects, values which are experiences, and values which are states of affairs. I propose to distinguish *private values* from *social values*. The aim of my discussion will be to establish three theses: First, the objects, experiences, and states of affairs which most liberal philosophers assume men to be interested in all fall into the category of private values; Second, there is a distinct class of possible values, called social values, which are not private values, or compounds of private values, or in any way reducible to private values; and Third, among these possible social values are the values of *community*, which taken together constitute a possible ideal of collective social action in a good society.

A SIMPLE PRIVATE VALUE is *a possible object of interest whose definition makes essential reference to the occurrence of a state of consciousness in exactly one person.* For example, suppose that I want the warm feeling that comes from a sip of good brandy. The definition of the object of my interest would be "the warm feeling that comes from a sip of good brandy," and obviously there is an essential reference here to a state of consciousness, namely that warm feeling. In general, any action undertaken for the purpose of producing pleasure (or pain) in myself or someone else qualifies as an action in pursuit of a simple private value.

Not all values are simple private values, although the traditionally liberal doctrine of psychological hedonism makes the mistake of supposing that they are. For example, when I try to start my car, the object of my interest is the starting of my car, and in the definition of that object no reference is made to a state of consciousness in anyone. Similarly, when I undertake to build a house, grow tomatoes, feed my dog (leaving to one side the occurrence of states of consciousness in dogs), or play the Beethoven violin concerto, the object of my interest does not essentially involve anyone's state of consciousness. Of course, insofar as I am deliberately attempting to accomplish some end, a state of consciousness must occur in me, for volition and intention involve consciousness, habitual action to the contrary not-withstanding. But it is one thing to say that the *intention* to produce X is a conscious state, and quite another thing to say that X itself is, or involves, a state of consciousness.

Many philosophers in the hedonist and utilitarian tradi-tion have claimed that as a matter of fact everyone always does what he does in order to produce a feeling of pleasure in himself, or at least to reduce or eliminate a feeling of pain. If this theory were true (and of course it is not, as Bishop Butler showed some time ago), then all values would in fact be private values, and indeed private values of a cer-tain specific sort. That is to say, the object of every interest would be—barring altruism, positive or negative—a state of pleasurable consciousness in the agent himself.

Since my concern in this essay is with possible values, not actual values, I shall decline the challenge posed by the psy-chological hedonist and simply assume that men sometimes take an interest in things other than their own states of con-sciousness. If I succeed in proving that there is a realm of possible *social* values which cannot be reduced to, or ex-plained in terms of, private values, it will be time enough to ask whether men are psychologically capable of taking an interest in them.

A *simple private value,* as I have said, is a possible object of interest whose definition makes essential reference to the occurrence of a state of consciousness in *exactly* one person. It might be objected that I have violated this definition in my very first example, that of the sip of good brandy. After all, the cooperation of countless persons is necessary in order to grow and process the grapes, make the bottle, and bring that sip of brandy to my lips. At every stage along the way there are "states of consciousness" in the persons whose deliberate activity contributes to the making and marketing of the brandy. In like fashion, the argument might continue, virtually all of the "private" enjoyments of modern life depend for their production on the contributions of numerous conscious agents. Hence only such simple pleasures as the smell of fresh air or the tingle of a crisp autumn day can possibly fall under the heading of simple private values. Indeed, even these are suspect, for the cooperation of many persons was needed to bring me to the point in time and space at which I smelled the air or felt the autumn breeze.

The argument is wrong in a very important way, for it plays into the classical liberal mistake of conceiving the relationship among men as purely instrumental or accidental, rather than as intrinsic and essential. The point is that when I want the pleasant taste of the brandy, *what I want is completely independent of the means by which it is at the moment obtainable*. It is true that brandy is man-made, but if (mirabile dictu) it flowed naturally from a spring or could be tapped from trees my desire for its taste could be satisfied without the cooperation of another human being. The question for our purposes is not whether it is likely that brandy should flow from springs, or suits of clothes grow on trees, but simply whether it is logically possible. If it is, then my desire for them does not *essentially* require the occurrence of states of consciousness in other persons. A Robinson Crusoe alone on his island could, with the appropriate technical assistance or divine intervention, enjoy all of the simple private values which we customarily obtain through the cooperation of our fellow men. Indeed, classical liberalism, insofar as it assumes that all values are private values, portrays society as an aggregation of Robinson Crusoes who have left their islands of private value merely for the instrumental benefit of increasing their enjoyment through mutually beneficial exchange.

Broad as the category of simple private values is, it obviously does not include all of the objects, events, or states of affairs in which someone might take an interest. Suppose, for example, that I close the window of a classroom in which I am lecturing in order to prevent my students from feeling cold. My object, in a manner of speaking, is to produce a feeling of warmth in Jones, in Smith, in Finkelstein, in Gordon, and in each of the other students in the room. The proper definition of the object of my interest, then, is "a feeling of warmth in Jones *and* a feeling of warmth in Smith *and* etc." Obviously, the definition makes essential reference to the occurrence of states of consciousness (feelings of warmth) in several persons, and hence the object of my interest does not qualify as a *simple private value*. Nevertheless, the object of my interest is a simple aggregation or summation of states of affairs which *do* qualify as simple private values. In that sense my object is *made up of* a number of simple private values, and so can be called a *compound private value*. Other examples of possible compound private values are:

1. a pleasant sensation in Jones and a sharp pain in either Smith or Robinson;
2. a sense of accomplishment in at least half of the graduating class of an elementary school;
3. the greatest happiness of the greatest number.

Drawing on some of the technical devices of recent analytic philosophy, we can define a *compound private value* as *a possible object of interest whose definition is a truth functional construct of definitions of simple private values*. In other words, compound private values are objects of interest whose definitions have some form as "p and q" or "p and q or r" or "p only if q" where the p's and q's and r's are definitions of simple private values.

As the third example above of compound private values

indicates, utilitarianism in all of its varieties concerns itself only with simple and compound private values. It assumes that the only objects of interest (or at least the only significant objects of interest) are states of pleasure and pain in one or more persons. It is in this sense that utilitarianism can be called "methodologically individualist," for compound private values can be defined in terms of, or are "reducible to," simple private values, and simple private values are values involving states of consciousness in separate individuals.

Leaving to one side those possible objects of interest which do not involve states of consciousness at all, what sorts of possible values are there besides private values? It would seem that any state of affairs involving consciousness must either involve *one* person's consciousness, or else it must involve an aggregation of states of consciousness in *several* persons. From this it should follow that all such values will be either simple or compound private values. Short of postulating some imaginary "group mind" with interests and goals of its own—a move rather unhappily familiar in the literature of idealist philosophy—we would seem to exhaust the logical possibilities when we define the categories of simple private value and compound private value.

To see that this is not so, let us begin by considering a very simple case: suppose that Jones hates Smith, and wants to see him suffer.* What precisely is the object of Jones' in-

---

* Many years of argument with sceptical students have convinced me that examples of human nastiness are vastly superior to examples of human niceness when one is trying to disprove the theory of psychological egoism. Strictly speaking, negative altruism is as much a contradiction of egoism as positive or benevolent altruism. "Altruism," after all, simply means "other-ism," or a concern for others, but for some reason sceptics are more willing to grant that men truly hate than that they truly love. Still, we may take heart in the reflection that once a sceptic has admitted that it is logically possible for one man to want another to suffer, he cannot very well deny that it is equally possible (albeit perhaps not equally probable) for one man to want another to be happy.

terest? It would *not* be correct to answer, Smith's pain, for what Jones wants is to *see* (i.e., to know about) Smith's suffering. Jones' goal or object, then, is *His knowing that Smith is suffering*. This definition makes essential reference to states of consciousness in two persons, viz. Jones' knowing and Smith's suffering. What is more, there is no possible way of translating the definition into a truth-functional compound of two definitions, each of which defines a simple private value. For example, one cannot say that Jones desires "Jones' knowing *and* Smith's suffering," for the crucial point is that Jones' knowing is knowing *that* Smith is suffering. He doesn't, for example, desire the compound private value defined as "Jones' knowing the capitol of Virginia *and* Smith's suffering," or any other such combination of Smith's suffering with an irrelevant bit of knowing in Jones.

The point here, of course, is that we are now considering states of consciousness which are, or involve, thoughts about other states of consciousness. Not all acts of altruism (positive or negative) have this complex structure, for sometimes the altruist merely wants the other to be happy (or unhappy), and in those cases the object of the act is a simple private value, a state of consciousness in exactly one person. But frequently altruists want to know that they have made someone happy or unhappy (hence the arrangement whereby charitable organizations put donors in touch with the recipients of their gifts). When this is the case, the object of their interest can only be defined by a phrase which does not reduce to a truth-functional construct of definitions of simple private values.*

Not every thought about another thought qualifies as an *Interpersonal Value*, as I shall call this new type of value

---

* The impossibility of handling intensional contexts by simple truth-functional composition is well known. I am simply making use of the fact for the purpose of elucidating the concept of a social value.

which we have just encountered. Let us define an inter-personal value as *a possible object of interest whose defini-tion makes essential reference to a thought about an actual state of consciousness in another person.* Then the do-good-er's desire to know about the happiness he has produced and the sadist's pleasure *in* another's pain would both be ex-amples of possible interpersonal values. But if Jones merely wants to daydream about Smith's misery, then his object is not an interpersonal value even though it is a thought about another's state of consciousness. The reason is that in order for Jones to get his wish, it is not necessary that Smith actu-ally suffer, but merely that Jones imagine Smith's suffering. (So a virtuoso hater might prefer to put off the torture of his enemy in order to enjoy to the full the contemplation of the event before actually performing it—it being easier to pro-long the imagining of torture than the actuality.)

Before we proceed to the analysis of interpersonal values, there is one major objection which must be stated and met. Interpersonal values, it might be argued, are not a distinct class of values irreducible to the class of private values. They are simply private values which include among their com-ponents the enjoyment which the individual takes in the *sup-posed* occurrence of states of consciousness in others. That enjoyment does not depend essentially upon the actual oc-currence of any state of consciousness in another person, al-though it may very well depend essentially upon the indi-vidual's *belief* that such a state of consciousness exists.

Consider once again the case of Jones and his malevolent attitude toward Smith. I have argued that Jones' desire is the complex state of affairs defined as "Jones' knowing that Smith is suffering." My critic, however, might reply that in fact what Jones enjoys, when his desire is satisfied, is his *belief* that Smith is suffering, not the fact that Smith is suffering. In proof of this, we need only reflect that there is no possible

discernible difference between the quality of Jones' enjoyment on the occasion of Smith's real misery and the quality
of his enjoyment when, let us imagine, Smith maliciously
mimics suffering in order to fool Jones. In retrospect, of
course, Jones may come to realize that he has been fooled,
and *that* realization (or more precisely, that *belief*) may be
unpleasant. But nothing can alter the character of the original enjoyment itself. So it would seem that the real object of
Jones' interest is the occurrence in himself of a belief that
Smith is suffering, and that, as we have seen, is a state of
affairs which need not involve any state of consciousness in
Smith at all.

Perhaps an actual example will make this point clearer.
Some while ago, I taught a course in problems of philosophy
at a well-known women's college. In the class there was a
pleasant, alert, responsive young lady who smiled at my
jokes, nodded intelligently at the more subtle points I sought
to make, and in every way gave evidence of having understood my lectures. On several occasions I remarked to my
wife what a pleasure it was to teach such intelligent students,
and I even delivered myself of the opinion that the true reward of the teaching profession is the achievement of that
state of communication in which one knows that one has
gotten across an idea to a student. At the end of the term, I
read this student's final examination and discovered to my
dismay that she hadn't understood a word I had said! Her
performance in class was simply a skillfully executed bit of
learned behavior designed to gratify her teachers and raise
her grade.

I want to say that I now realize I was wrong, that I never
in fact experienced the delights of successful teaching, and
hence that the object of my interest—that interpersonal value
called communication—was never actualized. But my critic
will object that I am confusing subsequent disappointment

with initial frustration. To be somewhat dramatic, if I had died before the final exam, there would be no conceivable ground for the minister delivering my eulogy to say, "His life lacked the enjoyment of the interpersonal value of successful classroom communication." Generalizing his argument, the critic would say that so-called interpersonal values are simply private values whose definitions make reference to *beliefs* about the occurrence of states of consciousness in others. Consequently, all of the possible values involving states of consciousness turn out, upon analysis, to be private values of one sort or another, even though the definitions of some of them make reference to beliefs about other states of consciousness. In short, man *is* an island entire unto himself, although he may hang the walls of his hut with pictures of other islands.

Before replying to this very powerful objection,* let me make two points by way of clarification. First, the problem has nothing essentially to do with the supposed difficulty of knowing about other minds and their contents. The question raised by the critic is not whether it is logically possible to know that states of consciousness occur in persons other than myself, but whether there is, for the theory of value, any legitimate distinction other than future consequences between an interest which is satisfied by a true belief and an interest which is satisfied by a false belief.

Secondly, the objection has a much broader scope of application than merely interpersonal values, assuming that it has any merit at all. Since it turns on the difference between reality and illusion, or true and false belief, it cuts as well against the descriptions we would want to give of interests in things other than states of consciousness. For example, suppose that I very much want to run a mile in four minutes. The object of my interest, I would say, is *my running a four-*

* Which was brought to my attention by Professor Kai Nielson of New York University.

minute mile. Therefore, in order for me to get what I want, I must actually run a four-minute mile. But my critic, by parity with his former reasoning, must reply that I need only *believe* that I have run a mile in four minutes. A faulty watch or a mismeasured course can provide me with a full and complete satisfaction of my desire, so long as they go undiscovered. The general principle behind the critic's argument is this: Any desire or interest, the definition of whose object includes reference to actual states of affairs, can be perfectly adequately satisfied by an object in whose definition are substituted references to the subject's *beliefs* about those states of affairs. The truth of the beliefs is irrevelant to the satisfaction of the interest and therefore is no part of the correct definition of the object of the interest.

I have two replies to the objection which I have just developed at such length. The first is *ad hominem* in character, the second speaks directly to the logical issue involved. First: to anyone who feels himself in sympathy with the original argument against the notion of interpersonal values, I ask whether he is willing to accept the extreme solipsism of valuation which is implicitly contained within it. Is there anyone who will seriously maintain that a concern for reality in all its varieties is reducible without remainder to a concern for the illusion of reality? Will anyone persist in the peculiar view that a life spent in interaction with the real world is, so far as the pursuit of one's interests is concerned, no different from a life spent on a neurosurgeon's operating table with electrodes stimulating the brain, or under the influence of an hallucinatory drug which engenders an ordered series of false beliefs? Grant me only that there is a value difference in kind between the illusion and the reality of a goal achieved or a desire satisfied, and I think I can successfully distinguish private from interpersonal values.

My second reply is that the objection is a *non-sequitur*, for it assumes that I am attempting to distinguish between the felt quality of the enjoyment of a private value and the felt quality of the enjoyment of an interpersonal value. In fact, I am only trying to distinguish between the *object* of a private interest and the *object* of an interpersonal interest. I maintain that when someone tries to bring into existence an interpersonal value, the object of his interest is a state of affairs whose correct definition makes essential reference to one person's thought about another's actual state of consciousness. It may very well be that we cannot tell, through an examination of the first person's consciousness alone, whether the interpersonal value has been actualized. But it remains true that it is one thing to desire that some state of affairs come into existence, and quite another merely to desire to believe that it has.

The easiest way to see this distinction is to consider the sorts of steps we would take to bring about our goal in each case. If I really want to run a mile in four minutes, then I will go into training, practice running, and make sure to lay down an accurately measured course. I will then get a good watch to time myself, and have a go. But if I merely wish to believe that I can run a mile, I may purposely be a bit careless in measuring the distance, and even buy a watch of poor quality in hopes that it will one day fool me. Such behavior may strike us as odd, though it is perhaps more common than we imagine. Some people, certainly, *do* wish to be fooled. That is why lonely women hire gigolos, and kings hire philosophers. But deliberate self-deception is about as much like honest error as mirages are like lakes. It is unfortunately characteristic of some philosophers that they tend not to notice the difference in either case.

III

Among the many states of affairs which fall under the heading of "interpersonal values," there are some which involve not merely one person's consciousness of another person's consciousness, but also what might be called *reciprocal consciousness*. For example, Smith may want to know that Jones is suffering, but he may also want Jones to *know* that he knows (and to know that Jones knows he knows, etc.). In short, Smith may seek what we call *communication* between himself and Jones. I propose to reserve the label *Social Value* for *any experience or state of affairs whose definition makes essential reference to reciprocal states of awareness among two or more persons*. A (possible) social value may, of course, include more than merely the reciprocal awareness. In the case just cited, Jones' pain is an element in the state of affairs as well as Smith's knowledge of Jones' pain and Jones' reciprocal awareness of Smith's knowledge. (We might take this example as an analytic model of what is usually called "gloating!") Nevertheless, what makes any object of an interest a *social value* is the inclusion in its definition of reciprocal states of consciousness.

As a further clarification of the notion of a social value, consider the relation of master and servant.* What does the master desire? What precisely is it that he takes an interest in? If he desires *service*—that is, the performance of some action or the satisfaction of some want which he would rather not attend to himself—then presumably he will be as content with a nonhuman device which performs the same service, and delighted with one which performs it better. So men happily use telephones rather than messengers, vending machines rather than food stands, and dishwashers rather than housemaids. But although a master may merely desire his servant's service, he may also desire the deference which his servant shows him. He may actually desire the experience of dominating another human being, rather than the performance which results from that domination.† If it is deference or domination that the master seeks, then a mechanical

---

* My apologies to Hegel.

† Once again I adopt the tactic of beginning with nasty examples.

device will not do at all. What he wants is the establishment of a certain sort of reciprocal consciousness between himself and the servant. He wants the servant to submit to his will *and he wants the servant to know that he is submitting.* What is more, he wants to know that the servant is submitting, and finally he wants the servant to know that he knows. Without this reciprocal awareness, the true master-servant relation does not exist. If through some accident or confusion the supposed servant actually thinks of himself as standing in some other relation to the master (such as that of economic equal trading work for wages, or religious disciple performing an act of self-mortification), then the distinctive quality of domination or deference is lost to the master, who fails to obtain the social value he seeks. It is for this reason that servants can frequently protect themselves against what is for them the *dis*value of submission by laughing covertly at their masters, cheating them, and in general denying inwardly the attitude of submission which the master desires and thinks he is receiving.

An identical analysis may be given of the social values of love and friendship, if we may now turn to more cheerful examples. Anyone who values friendship for itself values the occurrence of a reciprocal relationship between two conscious and affective minds. True love is not to be confused with even the most admirable altruism, for it seeks a certain sort of reciprocal affect, not merely the engendering of happiness in the loved one. (Indeed, a too selfless insistence on the happiness of the other is frequently merely a screen concealing a fear of genuine reciprocal awareness. To paraphrase a classic Nichols and May line, in such an affair there is pleasuring but no relating.)

As the example of the master and servant shows, the several persons involved in a situation which qualifies as a social value may not all take the same sort of interest in it.

Presumably domination is a positive value for the master and a negative value for the servant (omitting, for the moment, any consideration of the subtleties of sado-masochism). Indeed, some of the parties to a social value may not take any particular interest in it at all. I might desire communication with you, even though it made no difference one way or the other to you whether you communicated with me.

The example of love makes it clear, also, that many social values are states of affairs with no particular political or "social" significance, however worthy they may be of being actualized. The question arises therefore whether under the heading of *possible social values* we can find any experiences or states of affairs which might plausibly be the objects of collective social interest. More particularly, is there some social value or set of social values whose actualization can appropriately be identified as the public good, and which may therefore be viewed as the proper object of *the public interest?* If there is, then it will follow from what has already been said that such an object is *not* reducible to a private value, and so we will have proved that there is a legitimate, nonderivative sense of the terms "public good," "general good," or "public interest." Reverting to the terminology of Kant, we will have presented a *deduction* of those concepts.

The key to the discovery of the general good is the concept of *community*. The severest criticisms of liberal society, both from the left and from the right, focus on the absence of community in even the most efficient and affluent liberal capitalist state. Conservative critics bemoan the loss of tradition and look back longingly to an earlier age when men were bound to one another by feelingful ties of loyalty and trust; radical critics decry the reduction of all human interactions to the exploitative rationality of the cash nexus, and look forward hopefully to a time when work will unite men in cooperative production rather than setting them against one another in destructive competition. Voices from the right evoke the political immediacy of the town meeting, while a cry goes up on the left for participatory democracy. To this antiphony of dismay, the liberal sociologist replies with a statistical analysis of daily time budgets, tentatively indicating that city folk spend more time with other people each day than do rural agricultural workers.*

What exactly is it that conservatives and radicals alike miss in liberal society? Can we define more precisely the feelings, experiences, states of affairs, or sets of relationships that the conservative locates in a cherished past and the radical in a longed-for future? The answer lies in a certain class of what I have called social values, specifically in what I shall call *the social values of community*.

A social value, it will be recalled, is a value whose definition makes essential reference to reciprocal states of awareness among two or more persons. This reciprocity of awareness may be achieved through verbal communication, as in a conversation, or it may result directly from nonverbal interaction. Sometimes even a glance suffices to establish that reciprocity of awareness which, when the parties take an interest in it, becomes a social value. Most social values involve several persons at most, but sometimes large groups of people, even entire societies, enter into what can fairly be called a reciprocity of awareness. When this happens, I propose to call the state of affairs thus achieved a mode or instance of *community*. (Thus a *community* will be a group

* Albert J. Reiss, Jr., "Rural-Urban and Status Differences in Interpersonal Contacts," *The American Journal of Sociology*, vol. LXV, Sept. 1959, 182–195. The author begins with a reference to Georg Simmel's famous description of the differences between rural and urban life ("Metropolis and Mental Life"), thereby making it clear that he conceives his research as in some sense an empirical test of the conservative critique of modern society.

of persons who together experience a reciprocity of awareness, and thus *have community*.) The social values of community fall naturally into three major categories, viz., the social values of Affective Community, of Productive Community, and of Rational Community.

The major conservative criticism of nineteenth-century liberal society was the absence of the affective ties which supposedly bound men together in preindustrial society. Against the liberal ideal of society as a contractual association of egoistic satisfaction-maximizers who entered into the political condition for mutually self-interested motives, conservatives offered the image of a feelingful, nonrational natural community of men bound together by tradition and culture. To Burke, to Durkheim, to Tönnies, the instrumental conception of society was impoverished, diminished, a revelation of what had already been lost rather than of what remained to be won. The free man of liberal society was to them a pitiful creature, alone in a hostile world, alienated, unchecked in his ceaseless acquisitiveness by the conventions of society, prone—as Durkheim warned—to be driven by egoism or anomie to the final despair of suicide.

Edmund Burke beautifully captures this sentiment in some of his best-known lines:

> Society is indeed a contract. It is to be looked on with . . . reverence; because it is not a partnership in things subservient only to the gross animal existence of a temporary and perishable nature. It is a partnership in all science; a partnership in all art; a partnership in every virtue, and in all perfection. As the ends of such a partnership cannot be obtained in many generations, it becomes a partnership not only between those who are living, but between those who are living, those who are dead, and those who are to be born.
>
> (*Reflections on the Revolution in France*)

The participation in, reenactment of, and reflection on the traditions of a society may of course be a purely private value. One may enjoy them simply as works of folk art or as instances of the human story. Thus enjoyed, they have the same value as purely imaginary customs encountered in a romance, or as the practices of peoples long dead. Then too, one may adopt toward the traditions of one's own culture that detached interest which the anthropologist brings to his work. Viewing the rituals and practices of one's fellows, one may remove oneself from the exchange of thought and feeling, preferring merely to peer in at the window rather that become part of the feast. Thus enjoyed, the culture of one's society becomes an interpersonal value, to be sure, for its delight would be lost if one discovered that the images did not correspond to thoughts and feelings of living people. But still such an experience is not a social value. There is no reciprocity of awareness between oneself and the others.

Sometimes, however, men participate in the rites of their culture with a full awareness of the participation of their fellows, and a principal part of their pleasure comes precisely from the experience of *sharing* the traditions with others. Over and above the pleasure of the spectacle, and the voyeur's enjoyment, there is a mutual awareness of the common heritage. It is this mutuality of awareness, and not merely familiarity or habit, which makes participation in one's own traditions, however meager they may be, more satisfying than observation of the rituals of others, no matter how elaborate and aesthetically excellent. A man must be odd indeed who prefers always to be the accidental guest at another's family gathering!

The sharing of traditions and culture takes many forms, of course. Sometimes it is solemnized in rituals of passage, as in weddings and funerals and the celebration of national holidays. At other times, the singing of anthems or reciting of prayers achieves the desired reciprocity of awareness. So prone are men to develop affective community that even a group of strangers, thrown together by accident in a ship or train, will after several days create a little common history to which they can refer with pleasure as a way of affirming their relationship. The English philosopher Michael Oakeshott is surely correct when he asserts, in his brilliant attack on the rationalist temper in political thought, that men are incapable of relating to one another in any way but traditionally, and that every "rational" attempt to act without concern for tradition results simply in a clumsy rather than a graceful evocation of tradition.

Affective community is the reciprocal consciousness of a shared culture. It is not the culture itself; nor is it the purely private enjoyment which individuals may take in that culture. Rather, it is the mutual awareness on the part of each that there are others sharing that culture, and that through such mutuality we are many together rather than many alone. Men can deliberately choose to cherish their culture, and through that cherishing to bind themselves to one another. Insofar as a society sets itself such an end, it may be said (and each individual may also be said) to take an interest in the sustaining of affective community. It seems to me an appropriate use of words to call this interest a possible element in the Public Interest, and to call affective community an element of a possible general good. Here then is our first answer to those critics who say that there is no public interest save the summation of private interests, and that nothing can be a part of the general good save the goods of private individuals.

A second answer can be found in Marx's famous analysis of the alienation of labor in capitalist society. Man, according to Marx, is by nature a productive creature. He fulfills himself by producing, which is to say by embodying his thought in external nature in the form of objects which satisfy his needs and delight his soul. Every sort of productive labor, from the labor of the woman giving birth to the labor of the artist creating beauty or the craftsman shaping artifacts, fulfills and completes man by enabling him to confront himself in the product of his labor, and thereby to know himself.

But man is not merely a productive animal, according to Marx, He is essentially a *socially* productive animal. In opposition to the characteristic view of the nineteenth-century Romantics, Marx asserts that men naturally produce in collective (though of course not always cooperative) interaction with one another. The division of labor, which Adam Smith portrayed as a convenient invention for increasing productivity, is for Marx an essential characteristic of all human productive activity. The biological foundation for this division is the sexual differentiation of men from women; the most sophisticated manifestation of collective production is the creation of society itself, as a system of "collective representations" or image of reality.

In the celebrated essay on Estranged Labor, in the *Economic-Philosophic Manuscripts of 1844*, Marx rather abstractly explores the several ways in which the capitalist organization of production alienates the worker from his product, his labor, himself, and his fellow-workers. Attention is usually directed to the first form of alienation, that of the worker from his product, but for us the significant form of alienation is the last, that of the worker from his fellow-workers. If we translate rather freely from the dialectical obscurity and paradox of Marx's Hegelian language, I think we can make some very good sense out of the point that Marx is urging. There are, we may say, four distinct satisfactions which a man can derive from a bit of productive labor. There is, first, the satisfaction he gets from the object itself: relief from hunger, if he has produced food, shelter from the elements, if he has built a house, aesthetic enjoyment, if he has painted a picture or written a song. When the product is seized from the producer and used to satisfy needs which are not his and for which he has no concern, then his product is made foreign to him. When that product, in the form of capital, confronts him anew as employer and exploiter, then he may truly be said to have become alienated from the product of his labor. This, of course, is according to Marx the characteristic plight of the industrial worker in capitalism.

The second satisfaction of productive labor is the enjoyment of the laboring activity itself. Men enjoy even strenuous activity if it is purposeful, self-directed, productive, and appropriately demanding of their skills and energy. When that work is commanded by others, when it is fragmented so that its coherent purposefulness disappears from view, when it is exhausting and debilitating, then its satisfaction is destroyed. The laborer perceives his natural activity as unnatural and oppressive. It is as though a knife were to shrink from cutting or a racehorse from running. In Marx's evocative words, "The worker only feels himself outside his work, and in his work feels outside himself. He is at home when he is not working, and when he is working he is not at home." This too, Marx claims, is characteristic of capitalist work activity.

The third satisfaction of productive labor is the delight of coming to be oneself, and coming to know who one is, through the encounter with oneself embodied in the products of one's labor. Creative production, of food and clothing as well as of works of art, completes a man by permitting him to actualize his needs and thoughts in real, objective space-time. Just as the painter fulfills himself by putting on canvas what may originally be merely an idea in his mind, so the ongoing actualization of purposes and plans serves to confirm and define a man's self to himself. Erving Goffman and others have emphasized the importance of role-enactment in the definition and sustaining of the self's image. Marx would add that the transformation of nature in one's image *is* the way in which this self-definition is accomplished. Somewhat impiously (though also in keeping with the Feuerbachian tradition on which Marx draws), we might say that God is the only unalienated person in the traditional scheme of things, for He created the universe and then made man in His own image.

Finally, in addition to the satisfactions of the product and of the labor and of the coming to know oneself through the product and the labor, there is men's satisfaction in coming to know *one another* through cooperation in collective productive activity. Men frequently find that what is satisfying to do alone is even more satisfying to do in cooperation with others. I am not referring here to the pleasures of gregariousness. If I like to gossip about football and if I also like to refinish furniture, I may find it pleasant to do both at once. This would then be an example of what I earlier called a "compound value." (Not quite a compound private value, since the pleasure of gregariousness is probably a social value.) We may compare it, somewhat facetiously, to patting one's head and rubbing one's stomach at the same time. Only jugglers imagine that such accumulations of discrete activities constitute genuinely new forms of activity. I am speaking instead of the satisfaction which comes specifically from working *with* others in the pursuit of a common goal or the production of a collective product. When a group of mechanics or construction workers fix a car or build a house together, there is (or at least there can be) a satisfaction in the groupiness, the collective character, of the labor, quite distinct from the enjoyment of either the product, or the individual labor, or the coming to knowledge of oneself. That enjoyment in collective work essentially involves a reciprocity of awareness, for it cannot be found in even the closest symbiosis between a man and a machine. When large groups of workers, indeed even entire societies, embark on collective productive enterprises, they may take an interest in the creation and enjoyment of a reciprocal awareness in the work process. The society as a whole may deliberately set itself to organize the productive activities of the community in such a way that this reciprocal awareness is increased and strengthened. Such reciprocity of awareness, which we may call productive community, may also be viewed as an element of a possible general good. Here then is our second answer to those critics who assert that there is no public interest save the summation of private interests, and that nothing can be a part of the general good save the goods of private individuals.

Affective community and productive community are legitimate components of a possible public good, but they are not distinctively political in character. Any group of persons can develop, and can enjoy the sharing of, a common tradition and culture, whatever their relation to a political organization, or indeed whether or not they have any political ties at all. Productive community as well is compatible with a variety of polities, although as Marx demonstrated there are strong causal links between certain sorts of perversions of the work process and corresponding modes of domination and subordination in the political realm. Nevertheless, if we were forced to restrict the public good to these two forms of community, we would have little reason to claim that we had laid the foundations for an alternative to the political philosophy of liberalism. We must ask, therefore, whether there is any species of reciprocal consciousness, appropriate to entire societies of men, which can serve as an attractive goal of collective social interest and provide the framework for a new political order.

The answer to this question, I suggest, lies in that collective deliberation upon social goals and collective determination of social choices which used to be known as direct democracy, and which I shall call rational community. Rational community is not merely the efficient means to such desirable political ends as peace, order, or distributive justice. It is an activity, an experience, a reciprocity of consciousness among morally and politically equal rational agents who freely come together and deliberate with one another for the purpose of concerting their wills in the positing of collective goals and in the performance of common actions.

All discourse involves a reciprocity of consciousness, if by discourse we understand reply as well as statement. But not all discourse achieves what I am calling rational community, for there is discourse between masters and slaves or between private parties, as well as that discourse which is the public conversation. Nor is all public conversation true rational community, for much of that conversation concerns other matters than collective decision and action. I propose to reserve the name rational community for that reciprocity of consciousness which is achieved and sustained by equals who discourse together publicly for the specific purpose of social decision and action.

In order for such rational community to exist, each member of society must recognize his fellow citizens as rational moral agents and must freely acknowledge their right (and his) to reciprocal equality in the dialogue of politics. To be sure, good consequences for each and for all may flow from the dialogue; and there may be men sufficiently impoverished in their political imagination to suppose that such instrumental value is the only merit of rational community. But men may take an interest in the existence of the dialogue itself, and if they do, they will strive to create a political order whose essence just *is* that dialogue.

As we have already several times noted, a discourse is (or can be desired as) a social value because it essentially involves a reciprocal consciousness among several persons. A dialogue in addition requires the possibility of an uncoerced reply. Hence it takes at least two free men to conduct a political discussion. This is the meaning of the ancient paradox that a tyrant can never be free. By virtue of his domination of those around him, he deprives himself of the interlocuters without whom free discussion is impossible. Kings achieve freedom only when they converse with other kings. In that sense, a free society is a society of kings, and Kant was right to call his ideal moral community a kingdom of ends.

And now, finally, we have returned to the subject of our first chapter and can determine the true justification for the absolute liberty of speech and communication. The rationale for the free society is not, as Mill implausibly urged, that it accumulates a greater store of knowledge or more effectively satisfies men's private interests. The free society is good as an end in itself for *it is itself a social value!* So long as men mislead themselves into attaching merely instrumental value to the dialogue of politics, they will cherish it no more highly than any other means to their private ends. When its effectiveness diminishes or other values are threatened, they will be quick to abandon it, consoling themselves that the dialogue can always be resumed when the danger has passed. But if men recognize the value of the dialogue itself, they will defend it against its constant enemies, and perhaps even sacrifice their private interests for its preservation.

v

At the outset of this chapter, I warned that I would only attempt to prove the *possibility* of a general good. It should now be clear that there is a legitimate set of goals in which men can collectively take an interest, and which can appropriately constitute the content of a possible public interest. A society politically organized as a rational, deliberative dialogue, collectively cherishing its culture and traditions, and engaged in productive enterprises which are collectively enjoyed in themselves as well as for their products, can truly be said to have and to pursue a public interest. In such a society, needless to say, men will continue to have a full complement of private interests, many of which may conflict with one another and the satisfaction of which may bear little or no relation to the public good. The public interest I have sketched is not intended to eclipse or supersede private interests, but rather to complement and complete them.

But nothing I have said thus far can be construed as an *argument* for affective, productive, and rational community. The modes of community are possible objects of social interest, but they are also therefore possible objects of social neglect or even of social aversion. For the first two forms of community—affective and productive—no valid argument can be constructed. It is morally permissible that men should choose to shun the sharing of a common culture or the fulfillment of socially productive labor. However much I may myself desire these values, I can do no more than urge my fellows to take with me a collective interest in them. As for the value of rational community, an a priori demonstration can, I believe, be given of our absolute obligation to seek its actualization, but these essays are not the place to attempt so ambitious a task. Nevertheless, it is my hope that once men are persuaded of the *possibility* of aspiring beyond the liberal goals of distributive justice and the satisfaction of private interests, they will find themselves drawn to the ideals of community. It is shrewd of the philosophers of liberalism to insist that their world of private values is the only possible world. So long as they are permitted to maintain that fiction, dissatisfaction with the ideals of liberal society can be dismissed as a nostalgia for youthful enthusiasm or as a grumbling protest against the human condition. Once the ideals of affective, productive, and rational community are defined, however, we see quite clearly that the dissatisfaction stems not from the poverty of human experience, nor even from the poverty of political philosophy, but simply from the poverty of liberalism.

Index

196

Index